The Divorce
Mediation Handbook

Paula James

The Divorce Mediation Handbook

Everything You Need to Know

Jossey-Bass Publishers
San Francisco

Substantial discounts on bulk quantities of Jossey-Bass books are available to corporations, professional associations, and other organizations. For details and discount information, contact the special sales department at Jossey-Bass Inc., Publishers (415) 433–1740; Fax (800) 605–2665.

For sales outside the United States, please contact your local Simon & Schuster International Office.

Jossey-Bass Web address: http://www.josseybass.com

 Manufactured in the United States of America on Lyons Falls Turin Book. This paper is acid-free and 100 percent totally chlorine-free.

Library of Congress Cataloging-in-Publication Data

James, Paula.
  The divorce mediation handbook : everything you need to know / Paula James. — 1st ed.
    p.   cm.
  Includes bibliographcal references and index.
  ISBN 0–7879–0872–X (paperback : acid-free paper)
  1. Divorce—Law and legislation—United States—Popular works.
  2. Divorce mediation—United States.   I. Title.
KF535.Z9J36   1997
346.7301'66—dc21   97–4607
                                                                CIP

FIRST EDITION
PB Printing   10 9 8 7 6 5 4 3 2 1

Contents

93202

Protecting Your Children

Financial Fairness

Introduction

It was a clear, chilly morning in early October. Sam and Jane stood with me on the steps of the courthouse, trying to absorb the feeling of being divorced. A husky man with bushy brown hair, Sam shifted restlessly, his usual enthusiasm not entirely lost in the solemnity of the moment. Jane stood beside him, gazing quietly at the people passing by. Her dark red hair framed a thoughtful face. Sam and Jane had been married fifteen years.

Their moist eyes and tentative smiles suggested competing emotions: sadness, relief, and even a hint of excitement. Their life together had come to an end; their new lives awaited them.

Turning to me, Sam shook my hand. "I really do appreciate your help. This was a lot easier than I thought it would be."

Jane smiled. "We both thought we were going to end up in a huge fight. Doing it this way was so much better."

We spoke briefly about their children, and as they turned to leave, Jane added, "Thank you for your help—and for your patience," acknowledging the sometimes difficult journey we had traveled to reach this point.

As I watched Sam and Jane walk off, talking quietly to each other, I sighed with satisfaction, for I had helped them dissolve their marriage in a civil way—through mediation.

Working cooperatively and with my help as a mediator, they had divorced without destroying each other. Together, they had made sensible decisions and reached agreements based on their future needs, the realities of their lives, and their children's best interests.

Like many thousands of couples each year, Sam and Jane had discovered that divorce does not have to be warfare, that mediation offers divorcing couples a way to

- Maintain their dignity and mutual respect

- Cut their costs dramatically

- Protect their children from the pain of parental conflicts

- Allow both parents active roles in their children's lives

- Divide property and provide for support in a manner that reflects their own—not a judge's—sense of fairness

- Maintain their privacy

Sam and Jane's divorce had not always been friendly. When they'd decided to dissolve their marriage, they had retained separate attorneys, expecting an amicable legal agreement. Instead, in a flurry of letters between lawyers and heated court hearings, their friendly intentions had disintegrated into rancor, distrust, and retaliation.

Moreover, their children, thirteen-year-old Courtney and ten-year-old Kyle, began having problems. Kyle's grades dropped, and Courtney refused to see her father.

The legal fees mounted along with the tension and unhappiness. After four months of litigation, each had paid more than $10,000. Finally, Jane's lawyer, seeing how distraught and discouraged her client had become, suggested that they try a new approach: mediation.

Thus I met Sam and Jane when they came in for their first visit. As we sat around the table in my office, talking informally, they spoke about their anger, fears, and needs. While I acted as a neutral intermediary, each listened to the other's concerns.

When I raised questions about how their children were faring, Sam and Jane acknowledged that Kyle and Courtney had felt the pressure of their parents' anger and had begun taking sides in the fray.

"What do you think would make this divorce easier for them?" I asked. Sam thought his children would benefit from spending more time with him. Jane agreed, but she also thought that Sam shouldn't make remarks critical of her to the children. Such comments, she said, had angered Courtney.

As we talked about their children, I asked if Sam and Jane had ever worked with a counselor.

"We went to couples counseling for several months before we separated," Jane offered. "We both liked the therapist. Even though we didn't save the marriage, she helped us see the other's point of view."

"Do you think she would be a good resource for advice about Kyle and Courtney?" I asked.

Sam and Jane liked the idea and made an appointment with their therapist for the following week. Soon Sam was spending more time with Kyle, and Jane was encouraging Courtney to see her father as often as she liked. Both parents began monitoring what they said about the other in front of their children, avoiding negative remarks. Family tension was easing.

Meanwhile I met with Sam and Jane for several sessions to consider their children's future care and the division of their property. With me guiding them through the legal issues of custody and support, property and debts, we explored the possibilities. We thought about the children's schedules, looked at the incomes and expenses both parents would be facing after divorce, and considered what property should go to each.

When arguments threatened to erupt, I refocused the discussion on the legal issues, rephrased their statements in more neutral terms, and helped them listen to each other.

As our talks progressed, Sam and Jane regained enough trust to reach agreements that both felt were fair and reasonable. They then

consulted with their own attorneys to make sure that those agreements were legally sound. Although I provided information about
divorce law, only their own attorneys could advise them as to
whether their agreements were "wise." In these consultations, however, Sam and Jane remembered that they—not their lawyers—
would be making the final decisions about their divorce.

Jane's lawyer was concerned that Jane had agreed to let Sam
have an equal voice in making decisions about their children's education and medical care, and Sam's lawyer advised him against
paying so much support.

When Sam and Jane returned to mediation, we talked about
these concerns. As Sam had agreed to pay for half the children's
uninsured medical expenses, he wanted some control over when
and where they would be incurred. Jane saw his point, but she
wanted to decide what school their children attended.

As I offered options (Would Sam be willing for Jane to make educational decisions if she agreed to confer with him first? Would
Jane be willing for some medical decisions to be made jointly?), Jane
and Sam reached a compromise: except for emergencies and routine care, all medical decisions for the children would be made by
agreement, and Jane would make decisions about the children's education after consulting with Sam.

Sam recounted that his lawyer had questioned the amount of
child support and alimony Sam had agreed to pay, pointing out that
it was more than was legally required. But we had already discussed
that issue at length in mediation, and Sam felt comfortable with his
decision.

As we stood on the courthouse steps that October morning, Sam
and Jane appeared satisfied. In separating their lives, they had regained a cordial relationship and protected their children's future.

During the last decade, mediation has emerged as an increasingly popular way for couples to avoid the high emotional and financial cost

of litigated divorces. Rather than pay lawyers to negotiate the terms of their divorce, couples sit down with a neutral intermediary—their mediator—to discuss and agree on a fair and reasonable settlement.

Like Sam and Jane, they usually consult with separate attorneys on the side to make sure they aren't making foolish decisions, but they maintain control of their divorce rather than turn it over to lawyers and judges. They also avoid the adversarial nature of our litigation system; instead of fighting each other to "win" all they can, they cooperate to achieve a result both can live with.

Some couples come to agreements easily; others are hostile and wary with each other. But almost all work out agreements on their own, with mediators guiding them through the issues and helping them review their options. National statistics indicate that about 85 percent of all cases mediated are settled amicably in mediation. In my experience, the percentage is higher when couples come in before becoming involved in contested litigation.

Mediation is also less expensive than litigation, in part because it's less time consuming than having lawyers send letters, make phone calls, and argue legal points before a judge. Sam and Jane's mediation fee was about $2,500, and each paid his or her attorney only a few hundred dollars for consultations during the mediation. Compared to the $20,000 they had already paid in legal fees, mediation was a bargain.

For most couples I see, my fee is even less because they come to mediation before engaging in a legal battle. Once a couple becomes entangled in litigation, the cost of mediation is usually greater because they must first regain a civil relationship.

Even couples who don't resolve all their issues in mediation usually agree on many of them. That means fewer questions for their attorneys or the judge to decide and therefore less conflict and less expense.

Most important, children profit when their divorcing parents preserve as much as possible of the love and trust their children need. By working cooperatively, these parents avoid destroying the affection and respect they still feel for one another and set the stage for successful coparenting after divorce.

Parents who mediate also provide positive role models for their children. They demonstrate that adults can solve their problems by talking, listening, caring, and collaborating—not by fighting each other.

Mediation is not an alternative for everyone contemplating divorce. It won't work when one spouse feels unable to express opinions fully and fearlessly. It won't work when one unreasonably demands that the other give up valuable legal rights and refuses to compromise in the face of legal realities. Dishonesty can also sabotage mediation. If one spouse has made a habit of deceit (or the other spouse believes that to be the case), mediation may fail for lack of trust. But for most couples it's a much-needed alternative to the traditional approach that forces the couple to treat each other as enemies.

If you're considering divorce, I sympathize. Many years ago I went through a divorce myself. I had a four-year-old daughter and little knowledge of the world. I was frightened, inexperienced, and angry about my failed marriage.

Mediation was not available in those days. My husband and I simply turned our destinies over to our two attorneys and hoped they knew what they were doing. We didn't speak to each other about legal matters; that was for the lawyers to do. We didn't discuss our concerns or our daughter's needs, and neither did our lawyers.

Many thousands of dollars later we were divorced, but with resentment and distrust and no idea of how we would jointly raise our child. Our property division was a mystery. I thought it unfair that the division took into account some things but not others. Why? My husband and I never talked about it, never had the chance to hear each other's point of view and work out a settlement we understood and agreed on. We relied entirely on our lawyers.

After my divorce I went to law school and eventually became a family law attorney. For eleven years I helped clients get divorced in much the same way my attorney had helped me. And I'm afraid that many of my clients were as befuddled by the process as I had been.

Nine years ago I mediated my first divorce and experienced a revelation: in mediation, couples can safely and knowledgeably work out the terms of their divorce on their own. They aren't ignorant children who must be silenced while their lawyers do the talking. With the aid of a mediator and the advice of their attorneys, they can make their divorce an opportunity to grow, make peace, and prepare for a new stage in their lives.

I have now mediated more than five hundred divorces, and in doing so have developed a great respect for people's ability to marshal the best that is in them when encouraged to do so. I have watched them struggle to overcome their fear and anger, to talk to each other without rancor, to appreciate their own and their spouse's rights, and to call on their shared history of friendship and affection as they end their marriages with dignity and goodwill.

If you're facing divorce, I hope this book will encourage you to consider mediation. I urge you to read it through before contacting a mediator or lawyer. Then, if you do decide that mediation is the right path for you, read it again, chapter by chapter, as you progress through the stages of your mediation. It's designed to guide you through the entire experience: choosing a mediator, talking to your spouse about mediation, gathering information, understanding the law, avoiding the emotional pitfalls, and negotiating your agreement.

Occasionally I'll suggest exercises to help you better understand your finances and your children's needs, referring to the appendixes for helpful tools and information. By using these tools you'll be better able to mediate knowledgeably and effectively.

New clients often ask me what they can do to prepare for mediation. This book answers that question. But more important, I hope *The Divorce Mediation Handbook* will encourage you to try this new approach to divorce; in doing so, you and your spouse may be able to close this chapter in your lives with acceptance and a sense of fairness. You can then begin the next with your self-esteem and mutual respect intact.

Austin, Texas   PAULA JAMES
March 1997

Acknowledgments

Many people have shaped, informed, and supported this book. Tom Epley, my agent, provided invaluable help in editing. Alan Rinzler, my editor, added his keen eye and excellent suggestions. Dorothy Arnold, my legal assistant, carried more than her share of the work at the office while I concentrated on writing. My husband, Don Rogers, provided encouragement, support, and helpful advice. And a great many clients allowed me to share a private and difficult time in their lives as they taught me that divorce can be accomplished with courage, honesty, and goodwill.

I extend my grateful appreciation to all of you.

—P. J.

The Divorce
Mediation Handbook

Part I

Choosing to Mediate

1

How Mediation Differs from Litigation

Divorce requires a lawsuit. One of you must sue the other in order to dissolve your marriage. In doing so, you automatically become adversaries. The law says so.

If you choose to follow the traditional path through this adversarial system, you will each hire lawyers who will fight on your behalf like ancient knights, charging each other with lances. Each knight, highly skilled in the intricacies of jousting but untrained in other ways to resolve conflict, will try to win by seizing for his client as much booty (children and property) as possible.

You will stand on the sidelines wringing your hands while you watch the battle—and, of course, pay your knight a high hourly fee. One peculiarity of this battle is that the wounds inflicted don't appear on the other warrior; they appear on you, your spouse, and your children.

This is not a sane way to dissolve marriages. Were you dissolving a business, you would not follow this archaic pattern. You and your partner would visit an attorney together to discuss the terms and prepare the paperwork. Unless it was unusually contentious, the business dissolution would be accomplished without a lawsuit. But our legislatures require that *all* divorces be conducted as hostile encounters.

Mediation is an attempt to remove your divorce from the adversarial arena of the courthouse. Although you can't avoid a lawsuit, you can avoid the bloody battle. You can choose to sit down with your spouse and a mediator and work out the terms of your divorce fairly and sensibly. You can banish the knights and replace them with wise advisers who understand the value of an amicable divorce and with a mediator trained to help you reach a fair agreement with as little bloodshed as possible.

Two divorces I helped with, one as an attorney and one as a mediator, illustrate these two approaches.

The Story of Bill and Ruth

Bill came to see me a few years ago for help with his divorce. As he firmly shook my hand, I judged him to be in his late thirties. Tall and lanky, with curly brown hair and an engaging smile, he followed me down the hall to my office. His jacket and tie indicated that he was a white-collar worker, and his friendly blue eyes and informal manner suggested an easygoing personality.

As he sat down, however, I could see his agitation. Bill had just been served at work with divorce papers, which included a restraining order prohibiting him from abusing his children or hiding assets from his wife. He was understandably shaken to learn that his wife was not only divorcing him but accusing him of child abuse and dishonesty.

"What's going to happen?" he asked, looking at me as though I held the last life jacket on a sinking ship. I didn't know yet, but as I examined the documents he handed me, I began to get a picture of what we could expect.

Examining the paperwork, I saw that Bill's wife, Ruth, had retained an experienced family law attorney, Jack Wicker. Jack and I had battled in court many times; I knew him as a skilled adversary.

I saw that Jack had set a hearing on temporary orders in a week. (Temporary orders establish how the parties will manage their children and property while the divorce is pending.) At that hearing,

Jack would be asking the judge to give Ruth temporary custody of the couple's two children—twelve-year-old Nathan and ten-year-old Jerry. In addition, Ruth wanted Bill to move out of the house and pay her support until the divorce was finalized.

When I explained to Bill what Ruth was seeking, he was distraught. He wanted more time with his sons than the every-other-weekend our courts usually give a noncustodial parent, and the support Ruth was requesting was more than Bill's income justified. That meant we had one week to prepare for a contested hearing: seven days for me to learn the intricacies of Bill's family life and finances, his strengths and weaknesses as an individual, and everything good and bad he could tell me about his wife.

It also meant helping Bill understand the legal fray he had just entered, and preparing him for what lay ahead. Bill was scared. Like most people, he was very upset at the notion that he would be in court in a week, having another lawyer ask him searching and sometimes insulting questions, having his private life laid bare to public view, and having a judge listen to the sometimes tawdry story and pass judgment on it.

Bill was also scared of the cost. "Look. I make about $60,000 a year and Ruth makes about $40,000. We get by pretty well on that, but we haven't been able to save much. We had about $10,000 in savings," he commented ruefully, "but Ruth emptied that out to pay her lawyer."

With some apprehension, he added, "I know you're going to want money today, and I don't know where I'm going to get it." Embarrassed and concerned, he asked if he could pay me over time. I declined. I had learned that many clients quit paying when the divorce is over, leaving me with large, uncollectible amounts owing.

With a hearing already set, I would need at least $7,500 to cover my attorney's fees and probably more before it was over. Because Jack's restraining order prevented Bill from borrowing against his profit-sharing account at work, his only option was to ask his parents for money—humiliating for a man his age. While I waited, Bill went into another office to call his father and ask for a loan, which his father agreed to.

Bill also feared losing his family. He didn't want the divorce and certainly didn't want to lose his children. A father of the nineties, he spent a lot of time with his kids and had been very involved in their rearing.

"I don't want to become a weekend dad," he insisted. "I spend most of my evenings taking my boys to games and practices or helping them with their homework." He looked at me anxiously. "Am I going to lose that?" I had a lot of work to do before I'd know the answer.

I immediately began negotiating with Jack Wicker, hoping to reach an agreement about the children and spousal support, but I also had to prepare for the hearing in case our talks didn't work. Preparing meant spending several long sessions with Bill, talking to witnesses who could testify about his parenting history, gathering documents to prove his income and expenses, and examining the family finances. I would then have to organize all of this information into evidence and testimony.

I learned from Jack that Ruth didn't actually think Bill would abuse their children—Jack had simply thrown in that language and the part about hiding assets because it was the boilerplate on his forms. Although she wanted a divorce, Ruth acknowledged that Bill was a good father, and she was willing for him to have large periods of time with the children so long as she had primary custody. However, she would agree to such an arrangement only if he paid her generous support.

"Oh, and one last thing," Jack tossed off at the end of our talk. "Bill's having an affair with a woman at work, Irene Sutphen, and I'm planning to subpoena her for the hearing." Jack was clearly enjoying my silence as his grenade hit home.

Bill had not mentioned Irene to me. When I asked him, he acknowledged that they had gone out for drinks together but denied that their relationship had gone any further. His marriage, he said, had been deteriorating for about two years, and six months ago he began talking to Irene at work. She was sympathetic because she had just been through a divorce, and their friendship had developed naturally. He was horrified that Irene might have to testify in court and wanted to avoid that embarrassment if at all possible.

When I asked Bill about Ruth's history, he informed me, rather uncomfortably, that she had at one time smoked marijuana regularly and still did on occasion. I had the pleasure of passing this information along to Jack, letting him know that I would be offering it into evidence at the hearing if we were unable to reach an agreement.

As I began gathering testimony, I asked Irene to come into the office. A tall, striking woman with long brown hair pulled back from her face, she was clearly distressed at being dragged into this divorce. She corroborated Bill's story about the extent of their friendship, but I wondered how well she'd withstand the rapier of Jack Wicker's cross-examination.

I spoke on the phone to the boys' Little League coaches, teachers, and Boy Scout leaders, as well as several neighbors and family friends. All agreed that Bill was an active and involved parent. They were not, however, eager to testify, and I didn't want to subpoena them if I could avoid it. It would do us no good to put on the stand a witness who was angry about being there.

In talking to several of Bill's coworkers, I inquired if they knew anything about his conduct that would sound less than positive on the witness stand. A few vague comments about his going out for drinks after work made me more uneasy about what Jack might expose on cross-examination. I knew, of course, that Jack was talking to these same people, looking for blemishes that he could exploit at the hearing.

Meanwhile I also learned what I could about Ruth's history and reputation. No one other than Bill expressed any knowledge of her drug use. She appeared to be a competent employee and was active in her children's lives. One neighbor did say that she thought Ruth was standoffish and didn't seem very affectionate with her sons, but this testimony by itself would not be persuasive. Our case for Bill's having more than the usual time with his children would have to rest primarily on Bill's strengths as a parent rather than on Ruth's weaknesses.

Finances, however, provided more promising material. Bill looked pained as we discussed Ruth's spending habits. "Well, Ruth has expensive tastes," he began. "She's a great dresser and she's made our house a showplace, but she doesn't know when to stop."

Ruth had in fact run up a lot of debts for expensive clothes and household items, as was evident from the department store statements that Bill gathered for me. Our position became clear: Ruth didn't really need all the money she was asking for from Bill; she had inflated her budget to cover the cost of luxuries.

As Jack and I gathered our evidence, preparing the ammunition we would hurl at each other in court, we spoke at length on the phone. I pointed out the padding in Ruth's budget, her history of exorbitant purchases; he talked about Bill's relationship with Irene and his coworkers' innuendoes. I countered with Bill's commitment to his sons, his involvement in their activities; Jack countered with the high cost Ruth was facing to run the household after Bill moved out.

Our negotiations were heavily influenced by the "standards" that we both expected a judge to apply if we went to court. Local judges usually gave the noncustodial parent "standard periods of possession" (every other weekend and two hours on Wednesday evenings) and ordered "guidelines" child support (a fixed percentage of the paying parent's income). How much Bill would pay in addition for Ruth's support was uncertain.

As we hammered out an agreement, Jack and I both knew that if we wanted more than standard rights for our clients we would have to offer something of value to the other side. So, bit by bit, we increased our offers while insisting on something in return, each yielding as little as possible while wresting all we could from the other.

I ran our offers and counteroffers by Bill to be sure he concurred, but Jack and I were running the show. Bill sat on the sidelines, listening to my recounting of the negotiations, my evaluation of his chances, my recommendations for settlement.

In our bargaining, Jack and I were not primarily concerned with the needs of the children or their parents. We were far more influenced by the standard orders and how far we thought a judge might bend them in court.

Eventually Jack and Ruth agreed to let Bill have the children overnight on Wednesdays and occasionally on Thursdays as well; Bill agreed to give Ruth $400 more than guidelines support each month.

We reached a settlement Wednesday afternoon. I drafted the orders, which the parties and lawyers signed on Thursday; thus we avoided the hearing Friday morning. Irene didn't have to appear in court, Bill avoided testifying about Ruth's use of illegal drugs, and neither had to recount every sordid detail he or she could remember about the other. Bill and Ruth avoided spending at least a full day in court and paying their lawyers to do the same.

Although settling saved our clients a good deal of money and unpleasantness, the cost was still high. Jack and I had already run up $10,000 in attorneys' fees between us.

And we had just begun. The agreement we had worked so hard to achieve was merely for temporary orders. It governed only the period during which the divorce was pending.

Litigation is expensive because it's so time consuming. Talking to clients, witnesses, and opposing counsel; drafting motions and orders; preparing for hearings; appearing in court—it all takes a great deal of time. And, as I said, we had just begun.

When the divorce was finally completed ten months later, we had been through three hearings, several reams of paper, and a dozen office conferences with Bill and his witnesses. We had received many letters from Ruth's attorney that Bill found insulting and infuriating. And—even though we eventually settled without a trial—the total attorneys' fees exceeded $30,000.

Bill and Ruth's twelve-year-old son, Nathan, had begun disrupting class at school and harassing other students. He'd even slashed a neighbor's tires. Jerry, the younger boy, had withdrawn to his room, saying little to anybody.

By the time the divorce was finalized, Bill and Ruth were both deeply in debt, very angry, and distrustful of one another. Their children desperately needed help.

The Story of Terri and Eli

Now let me tell you about another couple, Terri and Eli, whom I first saw six months ago as mediation clients.

Terri called me to ask about mediation. A friend who had recently divorced told her how pleased she was that she and her husband had gone through mediation, so Terri thought it worth considering.

When she and Eli had decided to divorce, she visited a family law attorney but was dismayed by the retainer ($5,000) and the tone of the lawyer. "He said that Eli and I are now adversaries, that I must do everything I can to protect myself from him and to get as much money as possible." She paused for a moment, still apparently taken aback by the lawyer's advice. "That's not what I want. I'm sorry that our marriage hasn't worked out, but I'm not trying to take Eli to the cleaners."

As we talked further, Terri told me that they had a four-year-old, Melanie, and that their daughter's welfare in this divorce was the highest priority for her and Eli. She explained that her husband taught math at the university and that she had stayed home since Melanie's birth.

After Terri and I talked on the phone, I sent her some literature about mediation to share with Eli, and soon afterwards they made an appointment to come in.

When I entered the reception room, they were talking to each other in a friendly way and stood when I introduced myself. I could feel some tension in the air as we walked back to my office, but they were trying hard to be cordial.

Both appeared to be around thirty. Terri was small, with short, dark hair and serious brown eyes. It was summertime, and she was wearing shorts and a T-shirt, explaining that she had just dropped Melanie off at day care.

Eli was a tall man, heavyset and sort of sloppy looking. His fair hair fell into his eyes, and his distracted gaze suggested that he was more comfortable with mathematical formulas than with conversation.

After I talked to them about mediation and how the process works, we discussed Melanie—how they had cared for her in the past, what they wanted for her in the future, and how to best share her time and make decisions about her after the divorce.

Terri began. "Well, I've always taken care of her. I'm at home with her all day. I know Eli's a good dad," she added grudgingly, "but I'm her mother. She needs me." Having organized her life around Melanie's needs since the child's birth, Terri seemed apprehensive that Eli might encroach on her maternal role.

According to Terri, Eli had participated in raising their daughter when he was home, but he had not been very involved in her day-to-day care; she was reluctant to enter an agreement that gave him much of that responsibility.

Eli responded with irritation. "I know she needs you, Terri, but I take care of her too. I read to her, put her to bed, feed her. She needs me too."

Melanie was clearly the light of Eli's life. He proudly showed me a picture of her cuddled in his lap, her blond head looking like a miniature of his own. Eli didn't want to be relegated to a minor role in her life; he wanted to be a real father.

I asked both of them to talk about how they envisioned taking care of their daughter, at what times they each wanted to have her, and how they planned to make decisions about her welfare. As we talked, it became evident that they were not so far apart in their notions about Melanie's future care.

Sometimes fear and suspicion caused each to misunderstand the other and threatened to lead them into arguments; I would then guide them back to the topic, help clarify misunderstandings, and summarize in neutral language what each had said about his or her hopes and desires for Melanie.

For example, as we were discussing how they might share Melanie's care while Terri was looking for work, Eli volunteered to pick the child up from day care each day at two in the afternoon. His teaching schedule afforded him some flexibility, and he liked the idea of spending that time with his daughter.

Terri frowned. "That's not necessary. I can work my interviews around the day-care schedule," she responded uneasily.

"Maybe you can," Eli replied, "but you don't need to. It's easy for me, and it'll give you more time."

"I'm telling you it isn't necessary," Terri countered with an edge to her voice.

Eli looked hurt and exasperated. "Look. You've got to quit being so possessive. You act like I can't take care of her. She's my daughter too, you know. And I can take care of her as well as you can!"

"Well, you haven't in the past. You've just wanted to do what was fun and convenient for you. Now all of a sudden you want to spend all this time with her!"

I interjected: "Terri, it sounds like you're concerned that Eli may not be prepared to give Melanie the time and attention she needs, much of which you've given her up to now. Is that right?"

"Yes! I've always been there to do the stuff he didn't want to do. He doesn't know what it means to have the full care of a four-year-old!"

Turning to Eli, I asked, "Do you think it's true that Terri has provided the basic care for Melanie so that you could concentrate on your work?"

"Well, sure. I know she's spent more time with her than I have. And she's probably right that I let her do more of the drudgery. But I can do those things too! She's just got to give me a chance!"

In this way, Terri got to voice her anxiety about yielding some of Melanie's care to Eli, and Eli was able to reassure her that he was willing to assume the responsibility.

"I know, I know," Terri conceded. "I just don't want to move too quickly. Maybe we could try it once or twice a week and see how it goes."

Eli nodded eagerly. "Sure. That'd be fine!"

As we examined the parents' schedules and considered Melanie's needs, Terri and Eli gradually worked out a flexible arrangement for sharing their child's care and making decisions about her. They realized they would need to make adjustments when Terri returned to work and her schedule changed, but they began to trust that they could handle those changes cooperatively.

Eli, however, looked nervous about the likelihood that he would be moving out of the house. He reported that he'd talked to a divorce attorney who advised him that if he moved out he might lose rights to Melanie.

"He told me that I should stay in the house with Melanie if I want to make a strong case in court for having more time with her. I've been afraid that if I moved out, Terri wouldn't let me see Melanie when I wanted."

Once we had worked out a reasonable schedule for Terri and Eli to share time with their daughter and it appeared that they could agree on how they would make decisions, Eli became less fearful. He then relaxed and found it easier to talk about the house.

Both parents agreed that Melanie should be subjected to as little change as possible while she was adjusting to her parents' separation; because the child was used to being mostly with Terri, Eli agreed that it would be better for Melanie if she and her mother stayed in the house for now.

We next considered how bills would be paid during the divorce, as both were anxious about that issue. Terri pointed out that she currently had no source of income.

"Look, I'm not trying to make Eli bleed, but I don't have any other money. The mortgage has to be covered, groceries bought, utilities paid, and I need new clothes if I'm going to look for a job."

So the three of us listed all of their expenses, including what each needed for food, clothes, housing, and utilities. "Can you stop withholding retirement from your paycheck for now?" I asked Eli. "Can you make do with one suit for interviews?" I asked Terri. In this exercise, Terri saw just what expenses Eli was facing, and Eli saw the realities of Terri's situation. They both grappled with the limited income that was available to cover their bills.

Gradually we pared the expenses down to the necessities and worked out an arrangement for paying them, but it was clear that money would be very tight until Terri found a job; she needed to start looking as soon as possible.

Terri had worked in computer sales before Melanie's birth and hoped to get back into that field. However, she was nervous that it might take her considerable time to find a good job, and she didn't know how she would manage after the divorce if she didn't have work by then. After some discussion, they agreed that Terri would start looking for employment immediately and that they would not finalize the divorce until she had a job.

With those decisions made, I asked them to start gathering values for all of their assets—the house, the two cars, Eli's retirement accounts with the university, their bank accounts, and their household goods—and suggested ways to do so. We made an appointment for three weeks later to discuss child support and property division.

At the end of two hours, Terri and Eli looked relieved that they had agreed on everything that needed to be worked out immediately. They had every expectation that they would resolve the rest of the legal issues over the next few weeks. I asked them for a retainer of $1,500, based on my hourly rate of $200, explaining that if we didn't use it all, I would refund what was left; if we ran over that amount, I would ask for more later. They paid the retainer and left my office looking more relaxed than when they had entered.

As you can see from the stories of these couples, mediation differs from litigation in several major respects:

- Mediation is less expensive.

- Mediation is less acrimonious.

- The parties make their own decisions; lawyers and judges stay in the background.

- The parties work out support and payment of debts by examining their funds and options realistically and cooperatively, rather than by making accusations and demands based only on their own individual needs.

- Mediation is more creative and flexible. Instead of following the boilerplate provisions usually applied by lawyers and judges, couples arrange their children's future care and divide their property in accordance with their family's needs and their own sense of fairness.

- Mediation is private; the parties need not recount in an open courtroom all of the problems that brought on their divorce.

Yet in spite of these attractive benefits, mediation does not work for everyone. The next chapter helps you consider whether it's the right choice for you.

2

Is Mediation the Best Choice for You?

Probably 80 percent of divorcing couples are better off mediating; the others should let their lawyers negotiate for them. Although most couples can work out a fair and reasonable agreement with the help of a mediator, some are stymied for a variety of reasons. Perhaps one party is too intimidated to speak up or is unfamiliar with negotiating techniques. Another may be a bully—unwilling to listen to the other side's position. Or one may be ignorant about the couple's assets and unable to learn more without a lawyer's help.

In this chapter we'll examine some of these stumbling blocks to successful mediation and consider whether any apply to you.

Are Women Underdogs in Mediation?

Relatively new to the business world, many women are still learning techniques of negotiation that their husbands have practiced for years. Some people contend that this inexperience places women at a disadvantage in mediation.

This argument has validity; many women *are* uncomfortable negotiating. They often prefer the relaxed give-and-take of a "discussion" over the sparring implied by the term *negotiate*.

However, because mediators encourage a calm discussion of the parties' real needs and concerns rather than the jousting for position that occurs in "negotiations," they foster the kind of discussion more familiar to women.

Let me give you an example. Jack and Jill were arguing over who should get the last orange in the cupboard. After much clever debate, followed by a great deal of shouting and name-calling, neither had convinced the other to give up the orange. In resignation, they had decided to split it in half, when their mother entered and asked what all the fuss was about.

After hearing their story, she asked Jill why she wanted the orange. "To make a cake with the peeling," she replied. When asked why he wanted the orange, Jack explained, "to make orange juice." Once the children quit arguing for their *positions* and examined their real *interests*, both got what they wanted.

Negotiations too often consist of clever debate about each side's "rightness" and "wrongness," followed by shouting and name-calling. Mediation avoids this unproductive process by urging the parties to examine what they really want from the situation, not what they need in order to defeat the other side. Thus women's relative inexperience in negotiations may not be as big a handicap as it first appears.

Women as Negotiators

Nevertheless, it would be naive to suggest that negotiation never plays a role in mediation. When it does, the woman may be less comfortable than her husband.

Women and men often negotiate differently. A woman may have difficulty saying what she wants, and when she does she may understate her desires or simply say what she thinks is fair. Her husband, on the other hand, is likely to negotiate as he would in a business deal—start low and expect to move up as part of the ritual dance of bargaining.

"Have you two discussed how much Ginger should receive as a buy-out of her interest in the house?" I asked a young couple.

Jay looked at his wife. "How much money do you want?" His tone was impatient and tense.

"Whatever you think is fair," she responded.

"I think $5,000 is fair," he offered.

"Fine," she said.

Jay was ready to move on, but I could see that Ginger was not happy; $5,000 was not fine. She wanted more but didn't know how to ask for it.

"Do you think that $5,000 is fair, Ginger?" I asked.

"Well, we had an appraisal on it six months ago that showed we'd make $30,000 if we sold it. So I think $5,000 may be low." She spoke softly and uncertainly, looking quickly at her husband as she finished to judge his reaction.

"Well, why didn't you say so?" he said with more irritation. "I asked you what you thought was fair!"

"What amount do you think *would* be fair then, Ginger?" I asked.

"Well, $15,000 is half, so I don't know why that wouldn't be reasonable," she answered, her eyes glancing off Jay and back to me.

"What do you think about $15,000?" I asked Jay.

"That appraisal didn't take into account what it would cost me to sell the house, or that the carpet is old and the roof needs replacing," he explained.

"Is that right?" I looked at Ginger.

"Yes, but you're not planning to sell the house," she pointed out to her husband, "and the carpet and roof aren't that bad."

"OK, OK, I'll agree to $10,000, but no more. After all, I'll be taking over the mortgage, and I'm the one who'll have to pay for the repairs from now on. I ought to get some credit for that."

"But you'll also get all the increased value!" Ginger remonstrated.

"So, are you not willing to compromise?" Jay complained. "There's got to be some give-and-take here, you know."

Ginger looked confused. "But $15,000 is reasonable!"

In negotiation strategy, Ginger had started too low—she'd asked for what she thought was fair and left herself no room to negotiate. Jay expected her to play the game, to move toward the center, but she couldn't do so without abandoning a reasonable position. And Jay was applying negotiation techniques where they were not useful. His approach only confused Ginger and made her feel he was unreasonable.

I avoided a deadlock by moving to another point for a few minutes. When I found an issue on which Ginger could yield without compromising her sense of fairness, I suggested a trade—she could give in on this point, and Jay could agree on a $15,000 buy-out for the house. A deal was struck. Thus Ginger felt that she was treated fairly on the house value, and Jay felt that he'd negotiated successfully.

Women will do well to remember that they must be prepared to state what they want, and perhaps ask for even more, because men are inclined to negotiate. And men should remember that their wives may not really mean "Fine" when they say it and that typical negotiation techniques may not play well in mediation.

Women as Caretakers

Another concern for women in mediation is their tendency to be caretakers. I've observed many a wife torn between taking care of herself and keeping her husband happy. A man, on the other hand, is usually less concerned about satisfying his wife, expecting her to fend for herself. I don't make this observation to disparage men but to recognize that women are by tradition caretakers and often reluctant to make their husbands unhappy.

Men, of course, may also be caretakers, but when they are, they're more likely to act like a parent than a concerned equal or an anxious subordinate. A husband who has always handled the family finances may feel responsible for his wife's economic future. He may see his wife as incapable of handling her share of the community assets, and may attempt to "properly" manage them for her, even after divorce. He's often, but not always, generous in doing so.

Thus men and women who take on caretaking roles in divorce typically do so with different attitudes. Women may be preoccupied with their husbands' happiness and even fearful of making them angry, whereas men often want to protect and control their wives.

I remember Dee, a fresh-faced, twenty-seven-year-old woman who readily agreed to whatever her husband wanted.

According to state guidelines, Dee's child support should have been $650, but Sid, her husband, told me that they'd agreed on $450. I looked inquiringly at Dee.

She nodded. "That's right; $450 is enough."

As we discussed each issue, Dee repeatedly agreed to less than her legal entitlement. Finally, I halted the proceeding to point out that Dee seemed to be agreeing to whatever Sid wanted.

"I have some doubt about whether Dee is really expressing her own opinions," I commented.

"But we've already agreed on all these things!" Sid insisted. "Just ask her!"

Asking Dee did not yield any different results. She wasn't willing to express an opinion differing from Sid's.

"Why are you agreeing to less than guidelines child support?" I asked.

"Well, you know, he'll be paying off the mortgage so he won't have much money left over." (Sid would be paying the mortgage because he'd also talked Dee into letting him keep the house!)

Although I urged them both to examine Dee's financial needs and resources as well as Sid's, I couldn't force her to realize that her own needs were as important as his. I encouraged her to speak for herself but couldn't make her do so. Finally I insisted that Dee get legal advice, hoping that her lawyer could convince her to recognize and assert her rights.

My insistence distressed her. "But I don't want to fight with Sid! I don't want to spoil our relationship by making him mad. The money isn't that important to me."

I agree that people must sometimes make concessions to avoid fights, but I'm concerned when the concessions are all on one side. The imbalance suggests that one party is afraid to insist on her rights.

This caretaking role, often resulting from fear and lack of self-esteem, is likely to put a woman at a disadvantage in negotiating. If her desire to placate her husband overpowers her need to take care of herself, she may be bullied into a bad deal. On the other hand, if a woman wants to change this pattern of foregoing her own interests, she has several options:

- Become a stronger negotiator.

- Convince her husband to abandon his power struggle and examine their true mutual interests.

- Get a lawyer to negotiate for her.

The mediator is available as an ally in urging the husband to reconsider his position-based negotiations, but she cannot negotiate on the wife's behalf. The mediator is and must remain neutral.

Fear of making their husbands angry or unhappy is not the only reason that women sometimes settle for less than they could get in court. They may do so because they think that it's fair to accept less. Or they may want the divorce over with more than they want the best deal possible. These are valid reasons. But if you're complying with an unreasonable settlement solely out of concern about your husband's comfort, you may later regret your failure to assert your own needs.

When Negotiations Are Required

Many women, when confronted by an obstinate spouse, decide to "get tough" in divorce negotiations, to take stands they had been afraid to take before.

If you find yourself forced to negotiate with a stubborn and unreasonable spouse, consult with an attorney on the side. Your lawyer can suggest reasonable positions to take, point out options, and advise when to give and when to take a stand. With this advice, you'll probably be able to mediate without bringing your lawyer with you.

I remember vividly the first mediation I ever conducted. Both husband and wife had hired attorneys and begun the first steps in the litigation process when the wife's lawyer suggested they try mediation. They asked me to help, and we set about learning how together.

Jeff was a successful engineer who owned his own company, and Susan was a full-time homemaker with two young daughters still at home. Both parties were bright and articulate. Susan was bitter over the divorce.

"I helped Jeff build his business. I worked in the office for years, before we could afford to hire staff. I handled the books, worked with clients, and still raised the kids." Looking angrily at Jeff, she added, "Now that all of that hard work is paying off, he's decided he wants his freedom! You bet I'm mad!"

Susan had thought that Jeff's professional success would provide them both with economic security for the rest of their lives. Now he wanted a divorce, and she had no job skills and two children to raise.

Because Texas law didn't allow a judge to order alimony, Susan couldn't insist legally on anything more than her share of their estate and reasonable child support. But she felt entitled to more. She needed financial support while she developed skills for a good job.

Jeff, on the other hand, wasn't eager to give up the economic security that his success promised. Although he felt guilty about divorcing Susan and knew her argument had merit, he was reluctant to give up more than he had to. So it was up to Susan to argue her case—and argue she did.

Susan had strong feelings about her moral right to financial support and was very angry to boot. During our meetings, she fought fiercely for what she believed was right. Between sessions, both parties conferred with their lawyers. Susan's lawyer, a scrappy individual herself, prepared Susan well to argue her position, and she presented her case in mediation most effectively.

Although neither of them ended up with everything he or she wanted, Susan did prevail in gaining enough property and support to maintain her until she was prepared to reenter the job market. She probably got more than a judge would have given her had they gone to court.

I've seen similar results in many mediations—women who get more than they could have gotten in court, because either their husbands are generous and want to do what they believe is right, or the women negotiate effectively for a favorable agreement.

Bringing Your Lawyer to Mediation

If a woman wishes to pursue her legal rights and doesn't trust her ability to stand firm, then bringing her lawyer to mediation is another option. If one party brings a lawyer, the other will also, with the result that the lawyers may do most of the talking; however, the parties retain their decision-making power and thereby stay in control of the proceedings.

In this kind of mediation, we often "caucus"—the wife and her attorney are in one room, and the husband and his lawyer are in another. The mediator goes from one room to the other, discussing the case with each side and exchanging offers.

Even though negotiation plays a bigger role in mediations like this because the parties talk less face-to-face, the atmosphere is friendlier than that of a courtroom, and the process is substantially less time consuming and expensive than litigation.

If none of these mediation alternatives works, your attorneys may still try to resolve the case between themselves or in court.

Is Your Spouse Simply Impossible?

Occasionally I run across dysfunctional people who can't handle the give-and-take of the mediation process. These individuals usually display similar characteristics:

- They feel cheated no matter what they receive.

- They become incensed and emotionally out of control when their demands aren't met.

- They create scenes, threaten, and walk out.

- They frequently change their minds after making agreements.

Rita was this kind of individual. An attractive woman in her late twenties, Rita was studying interior design and raising two young boys, one from each of two marriages. Jerry, her second husband, had been married to Rita only two years before filing for divorce. Rita was vehemently opposed to it. Jerry offered her more child support than the state required and spousal support (alimony) for three years while she finished getting her degree. They had no significant property.

Jerry's generous offer exceeded the requirements of state law, but Rita fumed nevertheless. No matter what Jerry proposed, she complained bitterly about her lot in life and how unfair he was. Her first husband, she claimed, was equally callous. Soon I was added to the list of people who were trying to do her in.

Rita's exchanges with Jerry were so vitriolic that I separated them into different rooms to try calming her and keeping her focused on the legal issues, but she continued to fixate on the unfairness of her life. Rita soon gave up on mediation and refused to return.

Another example is Rickie, a successful and intelligent corporate executive in his late fifties. Rickie was very intense; he talked incessantly and became angry at any hint of disagreement with his own views. His wife of thirty years, Charmaine, was an emotional basket case, afraid to do anything that might anger Rickie. She cried easily and had trouble making decisions, particularly if she thought Rickie might disagree.

Rickie had all of his paperwork in order when we began mediation, and set about explaining to me just how the property would be divided. I had to ask him to slow down, as he was going so quickly through the numbers and making so many assumptions that I couldn't follow him, and neither could Charmaine. He was impatient with my questions, suspecting a challenge to his plan.

When I pointed out that Charmaine could not evaluate his proposal without more information, he became furious. He complained that his excessive generosity was unappreciated, and threatened to leave Charmaine nothing if she didn't agree to his proposal. In these scenes, Charmaine usually cried and capitulated, but to little avail. Rickie would return to the next session with yet more demands.

Throughout the mediation, I urged both parties to confer with their attorneys, but Rickie opposed having lawyers involved, and Charmaine didn't want to anger her husband. Finally, I *insisted* that Charmaine confer with an attorney before they made any final decisions. Rickie, furious, threatened to sue me. Charmaine, after more resistance, did see a lawyer, who convinced her to forego mediation and proceed with traditional litigation.

If one person in a marriage has been physically or emotionally abusive, mediation may not be the best way to divorce. If your spouse has abused or intimidated you to the point that you can't stand your ground without fear of retaliation, have a lawyer negotiate for you.

What If You Know Nothing About Your Assets and Debts?

Sometimes a client is nervous about mediating because he or she— usually she—knows little or nothing about the community estate.

Her husband may own his own business or have managed their affairs without her participation. Understandably she feels uncomfortable and at a disadvantage in discussing how they should divide their property.

If this couple were in litigation, the wife's lawyer would send the husband or his attorney a formal request for documents, with questions regarding their property and financial affairs, to be answered under oath. We call this process *discovery*. The wife's lawyer demands copies of all of the couple's business and bank records, tax returns, and anything else that gives evidence of their financial condition.

The problem is that lawyers, to be safe, ask for every document that could conceivably be relevant, such as all bank and corporate records for the last five years, even though much of it may be unnecessary. Then the lawyers and their clients must spend many hours gathering all the documents requested, answering questions, and reviewing piles of material.

Increasingly of late, one side attempts to avoid full disclosure by responding with clever and evasive answers. A judge then holds hearings and orders further discovery.

Mediation avoids this arduous and expensive process: each party voluntarily provides information that the other needs. If the parties are not certain what documents they need, their attorneys can help them draw up lists to bring to mediation. When the documents are produced, the parties may want their lawyers to review them. Only when one spouse refuses to provide needed documents does the other turn to formal discovery, but this is rare.

A wife sometimes asks me, "What if he's hiding assets?" The only remedy I know for this kind of dishonesty, other than hiring a detective to ferret out the truth, is to require the spouses to sign inventories that they swear are true and complete. Obviously, either could be lying. But if one spouse deliberately hides assets, it's the same as lying in court, and the other can sue.

In the situations described here—a wife unable to negotiate effectively with her husband, an emotionally dysfunctional spouse, or one refusing to disclose vital information to the other—mediation may not be the best choice. Yet I urge you to try it before deciding against it. Many couples who have doubts when they begin find that they can work through the obstacles, especially when their only alternative is long, expensive, painful litigation.

3

Choosing a Mediator

N ot every mediator is competent or right for you. In this chapter, I'll review what qualifications to seek, where to look for the right mediator, what questions to ask, and what fees to expect.

Some mediators are attorneys, and some come from other fields, such as mental health and the clergy. In some communities, lawyers dominate the profession; in others social workers, psychologists, and clerics may do most of the family law mediations.

Because this is a new profession and has developed differently in different areas, we still see great variety in how mediation is practiced and by whom. This chapter helps you anticipate those different styles and find the right person and method for you.

Qualifications

What should you look for in a mediator? Training, experience, and knowledge of family law.

Training as a Mediator

Whereas attorneys and mental health professionals must attend graduate school and pass state exams, no such licensing exists for mediators. Ours is a new profession, still struggling to develop certification standards. However, because mediators and bar associations in most states are now crafting such requirements, we'll no doubt see them enacted soon.

In the meantime you'll have to look to other criteria to evaluate a mediator. Training courses are one indication of a mediator's competence. These classes teach prospective mediators to help their clients focus on the legal issues, listen to each other's point of view, and examine their own positions realistically. Prospective mediators also learn techniques for resolving impasses, and study law relevant to divorce and mediation.

In my home state, a family law mediator is expected (but not legally required) to take a forty-hour course in mediation plus a twenty-four-hour course specifically related to family law disputes. Most other states expect similar training.

When you interview a potential mediator, ask how many hours of training she has received and whether it included instruction in family law.

Mediation Experience

Besides training, your mediator should have experience mediating divorces. The more, the better. Fewer than twenty mediations is considered beginning level; more than one hundred is considered expert.

Although divorce mediation is a rapidly growing field, you may find it difficult to find experienced mediators in rural areas and small towns. If so, try to locate one in the nearest city.

Family Law Experience

If you and your spouse plan to attend mediation without your lawyers, you'll want a mediator well versed in family law, for she'll need to guide you through the relevant legal issues. If the mediator is a lawyer, ask whether she has practiced family law and for how long. If she's not an attorney, ask about her experience in family law. How great is her knowledge, and how did she gain it?

Although she can't give legal advice, your mediator can make sure that you and your spouse discuss and agree on all the pertinent legalities. A mediator not experienced in family law may fail to raise important issues. For example, whose responsibility will it be to get the children from one parent's home to the other? What payments, if any, would a wife receive from her husband's pension if he dies before retiring?

Many people think that a lawyer is a lawyer, that anyone with a law degree is qualified to help them with any legal matter. This is not true, particularly in family law, which has become so complicated that most lawyers either concentrate in it or avoid it altogether.

As I discuss later, you may use a mental health professional or cleric as a mediator; but if you choose a lawyer, I strongly recommend using one who has practiced family law for many years. On the other hand, if you decide to mediate with your lawyers present, using a mediator who's not a family law attorney is feasible, because your lawyers will provide legal expertise.

Different Styles of Mediation

In my area, the practice of mediation began when attorneys who couldn't settle their cases asked an outside lawyer to help them reach an agreement. Typically, the lawyers who couldn't agree went with their clients to this third attorney's office for a full day of mediation.

Sometimes judges initiated mediation. Aware that this new approach was settling cases, some judges—especially those faced with congested dockets—began sending many of their cases to mediation.

A formal procedure developed. The two lawyers, with their clients present, described to their mediator the issues in dispute and their clients' positions. The mediator then either encouraged the parties to negotiate face-to-face or moved them into separate rooms and shuttled between the two, exchanging offers and generally abetting the negotiation process.

In cases not involving family law, this format is still the one normally used. But in divorce and other family law cases, lawyers, therapists, and couples have experimented with a variety of mediation styles.

When some divorce lawyers realized that their clients wanted to avoid the cost of paying them to attend mediation sessions, they suggested that their clients meet alone with a mediator. As more couples resolved disputes efficiently and inexpensively this way, lawyers sensitive to their clients' desire to contain costs increasingly recommended mediation without lawyers present.

Soon mediators began advertising for clients rather than waiting for lawyers or judges to send business to them. Thus many couples entering mediation now do so without having first seen an attorney of their own to advise them, and they may be able to complete their divorce without ever conferring with independent counsel. (Remember, the mediator is neutral, so even if she is a lawyer, she cannot give legal advice.)

This possibility that couples divorcing through mediation may not be receiving legal advice troubles many family law attorneys, not only because their client base diminishes but because they're justifiably concerned that people are getting divorced without receiving advice regarding their legal rights.

Styles of mediation also vary in terms of how mediators define their role. Many mediators who have mediated only with lawyers present view their own task as quite limited. Because their clients are attended by their attorneys, these neutral mediators may believe that mediation should merely provide a safe environment for negotiations. If so, they may be reluctant to suggest options, provide legal information, or comment on the positions of their clients. Indeed, some lawyers disapprove of mediators who comment in any way on their cases.

On the other hand, mediators who have successfully mediated without the parties' lawyers attending are more comfortable offering options, sharing necessary legal information, and helping clients evaluate their positions.

Even these flexible mediators, however, usually avoid stating what they think is "fair" and "right," because doing so may be tantamount to giving advice or taking sides. Attorney-mediators are particularly sensitive to maintaining their neutrality.

When you interview mediators, ask about their philosophy of mediation and how they envision their roles. If you've already come to a complete agreement with your spouse and simply want someone to draw up the paperwork, how a mediator defines his role may not seem important to you. But if you expect that the two of you won't agree on some issues or that there will be legal matters you need to understand more thoroughly, you'll want to know ahead of time how much guidance the mediator is willing and competent to provide.

Mental Health Professionals as Mediators

Therapists also mediate divorces, working with and without lawyers present. Not surprisingly, their style of mediation differs from that of lawyers. Whereas a lawyer usually concentrates on moving efficiently through legal matters, a therapist may focus on exploring the emotional dynamics of a couple to improve their communication. Also, therapists may be less cautious about guiding clients in a direction that the therapist considers fair.

Although attorney-mediators have the advantage of being able to draft the complex legal documents required, they aren't always able to guide their clients through the emotional mine fields that may strew the path to resolution. In these cases, a mental health expert can be invaluable.

Emotionally difficult cases are more common when couples have first tried litigating their divorce. Having been through contentious discovery and hearings, they may be so antagonistic and distrustful that mediation is very difficult. If they were hostile before litigation began, all the worse.

In such cases, a therapist and a family law attorney-mediator working together may be the best hope for settlement. If you're mediating with an attorney-mediator and are stuck in an emotional deadlock with your spouse, talk to your mediator about getting a therapist to help. If you and your spouse consulted earlier with a marriage counselor, you might invite him to participate in your mediation.

Using a therapist as mediator with a lawyer present to provide legal information can also be effective, particularly when emotional issues threaten to sabotage agreement. In this situation the therapist leads the discussions, and the lawyer's role is to raise legal points when necessary, record the agreement, and prepare the required legal documents.

Both of these approaches have the disadvantage of costing more because two professionals are involved rather than one. But it's worth the cost to have a therapist participate if his intervention enables you and your spouse to reach an agreement.

Many therapists mediate without having lawyers present and do an excellent job. The mediator will ultimately need to describe your agreement to a lawyer, who must then translate it into legalese. Although this process is a bit more cumbersome, it's worth it if your therapist-mediator is effective.

If you're considering a therapist-mediator, ask about his experience in family law. It's important that your mediator understand the intricacies of state law affecting divorce; otherwise, he will fail to raise issues that must be addressed in your legal documents, incurring additional mediator and legal fees to correct.

Clerics as Mediators

Because churches generally disapprove of divorce, they've become involved in divorce mediation slowly. However, some now recommend or offer this service, and many clerics have become excellent mediators. Their training as peacemakers and their sensitivity to the spiritual issues inherent in marriage and divorce prepare them particularly well to guide couples through this difficult transition.

Many of my comments regarding mental health professionals apply equally to clerics. They may mediate jointly with attorney-mediators or on their own, communicating the couple's agreement to lawyers for drafting. As with any other mediator, ask about the individual's experience in family law and mediation.

If you would like to mediate with a cleric, ask your minister for references.

Sources of Names

I've listed here many sources for mediators' names, but use your imagination as well. These suggestions are only starting points.

The Yellow Pages

Perhaps the best place to begin, the Yellow Pages is an excellent source for mediators. They're listed in two places—under "Attorneys" and under "Mediation Services." The attorney section will be quite long, and you'll have to hunt through the display ads for any mention of mediation. The mediation services section will probably be short, but an active mediator is almost certain to have an ad there.

Your Attorney

If you're already working with a family law attorney, she can probably guide you to a good mediator or at least suggest names for you to consider. Ask what she knows about the qualifications and style of any mediator she recommends, including the following questions:

- Has she mediated cases with this individual before?

- Were the cases settled successfully?

- Is the mediator experienced in family law as well as in mediation?

- Is he willing to mediate without lawyers present?

- Does he offer options and discuss legal requirements?

- What's his hourly rate?

The County Bar Association

County bar associations are beginning to include attorney-mediators in their referral service; some even have a separate listing of family law mediators. When you call, also ask whether the association screens attorney-mediators to ensure they are members of the bar and carry malpractice insurance.

Word of Mouth

Many people learn of mediation through a friend or family member. Ask around for anyone who has worked with a family law mediator. Most people who have are eager to talk about their experience.

Ask if the mediator was fair and impartial, if the fee was reasonable, and if the mediation was conducted professionally and efficiently. Did the mediator know the necessary law? Was he effective at helping resolve disagreements? Would your friend recommend him?

The Dispute Resolution Center

Many major cities now provide dispute resolution centers to help citizens resolve disagreements through mediation. Because the names of these centers vary, call your county and city governments and describe the services you seek.

Supported by taxes and charitable contributions, these centers normally charge nominal fees for their services. However, because these organizations were created primarily to resolve disputes between neighbors and between consumers and retailers, their mediators—often volunteers—may have scant knowledge of family law.

If you do decide to use a dispute resolution center, your legal paperwork must still be prepared by a lawyer, who may recommend that you return to mediation to resolve questions not addressed.

Your Therapist

Therapists are often knowledgeable about family law mediators, so if you've been seeing a therapist, ask him for a referral. If you don't know a therapist, you might ask friends for the names of therapists who work with couples. Such individuals are usually familiar with mediators and attorneys who handle divorce, and can recommend someone they've heard good things about.

The Courthouse

Many county courthouses now provide lists of mediators and disclose information about their training, experience, and legal specialties. When you call the district clerk's office at your county courthouse to ask about mediators, the clerk may use the term *alternative dispute resolution* or *ADR* instead of mediation. ADR is the term adopted by the legal profession to describe mediation, arbitration, and other methods of settling disputes that don't require court hearings.

Advertising

Check your local newspapers; mediators are beginning to advertise there. Anyone willing to pay the high cost of such advertising is serious about her practice.

On-Line Search

If you have on-line services, use "divorce" and "mediation" as search words in exploring the Web. You may come across the names of family law mediators in your area, as well as useful information regarding their experience, orientation, and fees. You may be able to e-mail them questions about their practice.

Some county courthouses now have web pages that include the names of approved attorneys and mediators. Search for your county's name on the Web.

Interviewing Mediators

When you have the names of a few mediators, interview them on the phone. You may even want to meet them before choosing one. Because some mediators discount their rate for the first session, ask about this before scheduling an appointment.

Most mediators will be happy to talk to you on the phone about their services. If a mediator doesn't return your call within twenty-four hours, I suggest you strike that individual from your list. You don't want a mediator who doesn't take care of business promptly.

When you do interview a potential mediator, ask about the following:

- Her experience in family law—I recommend at least five years of intensive family law experience if you plan to mediate without your lawyers present.

- Her experience mediating family law cases—I recommend at least twenty.

- Her formal training as a mediator. She should have at least forty hours of training, and twenty-four hours of instruction in family law.

- Whether she's willing to provide legal information, suggest options, and give case evaluations.

- Her hourly rate.

The Mediator's Fee

What a mediator charges will vary depending on her experience and professional background as well as on the size of your community.

Lawyers usually charge higher rates than therapists, but they may be more efficient (and therefore less expensive in the end) because there is less duplication of work. They don't have to translate your agreement to an attorney who was not present at the mediation and who may not understand all the nuances of your settlement. You thus avoid repeated drafts and meetings to iron out problems.

Ask mediators you interview if they can estimate the *total* cost of your mediation—including the fee of the mediator and of other experts you may need to consult.

Sometimes potential clients expect mediators to quote flat fees. I don't know of any family law mediator who does so, because he can't predict how long a mediation will take. The *average* cost of my mediations is $1,200, but if I charged everyone that amount, couples with simple estates and cooperative attitudes would be subsidizing those with complex property issues or who are embroiled in bitter disputes.

Hourly Rate

In my community, family law attorneys charge between $100 and $300 an hour, depending on their years of experience and their standing in their professional community. Therapists charge between $75 and $150 an hour, depending on the same criteria. (My hometown has a population of about half a million people. Fees are usually lower in smaller cities and higher in larger ones.)

An experienced mediator knowledgeable about family law will charge more than one less qualified, but he'll be more valuable to you and more efficient in conducting the mediation. You'll benefit by his years of experience, even if you and your spouse have a simple mediation.

Also keep in mind that many couples underestimate the complexity of their divorces. Some couples tell me at our first session that they've reached an amicable agreement on all aspects of their divorce and therefore expect a brief and simple mediation. Sometimes they do have such an agreement, but sometimes not. When couples attempt in mediation to tie down the details of child support, custody, who gets what property, and who's responsible for various debts, they frequently discover they agree less than they'd thought.

Retainers

Another advantage of mediating is that you avoid paying the sizeable retainers required by lawyers who litigate divorces. In my area, most experienced family law attorneys ask for retainers of at least $2,000 to $3,000—more if the divorce offers any complications. Thus couples who litigate can expect to pay a total of at least $5,000, even if their divorce is simple and amicable. Because mediation costs less, mediators require smaller retainers—if they require them at all.

If your mediator does require a retainer, be sure you have a written agreement with him that he will refund any unused portion to you and your spouse.

Free and Reduced-Fee Mediations

Most mediators feel an ethical obligation to provide free or reduced-fee services for couples with very limited incomes and assets. If you think you might fit into this category, check when interviewing mediators to see if they'll work with you on this basis.

4

The Role of the Mediator

Getting divorced is like driving on the freeway in a fog so thick that you can't see more than a few feet in any direction. The decisions you make are crucial; a mistake can cause serious damage. But because you can't see the other cars or the road ahead, you don't know which way to turn. You're likely to end up yelling at the person in the passenger seat, who is just as scared as you are and no more able to see clearly.

Couples going through divorce are often caught up in a fog of emotional turmoil. They can't think clearly. They can't see possibilities crucial to their well-being. They're so hurt and angry that rational discourse doesn't have a chance.

The mediator is like a driving instructor helping you navigate. Standing outside the fog, he watches your progress, points out when you're about to go off the road or run into another car, and guides you through the treacherous turns on your way home. He also helps you make reasonable choices in a cooperative atmosphere rather than in one rife with demands and accusations.

Although the mediator has many tricks of the trade he uses to get you through the fog, his role is limited—there are things he can do and things he can't.

Stays Neutral

The definition of a mediator usually reads something like this: "The mediator is a neutral third person who helps disputing parties reach an agreement."

Neutrality is essential. If either side believes the mediator is biased, she'll lose her effectiveness in resolving disputes. She must treat each side impartially.

In the early days of my mediation career, a wife wanted to see me alone before the couple came in together. The husband didn't object, so the wife and I met and discussed the issues in their divorce.

Unfortunately, when I later saw them together, the husband regarded me as biased in her favor, and I was unable to change his perception. Though they eventually settled their differences in mediation, it was a longer and more contentious experience because of his distrust. Thus, as I learned, the mediator must not only avoid bias but also steer clear of any *appearance* of bias.

Maintaining neutrality also means that the mediator can't be a legal representative of either side. Therefore, neither party's lawyer can act as mediator. Because your attorney's job is to safeguard *your* interests, he is by definition biased in your favor. If he's not, he's not doing his job.

If the mediator has had any prior dealings with one side, she must disclose that fact to the other, who can then decide whether to continue with her as mediator.

Neutrality also means that the mediator can't give legal advice, even if she's an attorney. So what is legal advice? The answer to that question is unclear. Suggesting what a party should or shouldn't agree to is certainly prohibited as legal advice. But what if the mediator describes for a couple the statutory guidelines for child support? Or points out that an arrangement to which they've agreed is contrary to local court rules? I regard this kind of data as legal *in-*

formation—not legal advice—and therefore proper for a mediator to discuss. Indeed these facts are essential to a couple if their lawyers aren't present. However, some mediators may disagree. I'll discuss these differences of opinion more fully in the next chapter.

The mediator's neutrality also makes it awkward for her to "protect" one party from the other. If your spouse is a bully, it's not the mediator's job to shield or defend you. She may, however, insist that you get legal advice so that your lawyer *can* provide protection.

Helps You Make Your Own Decisions

In mediation, you make your own decisions—the mediator doesn't make them for you. To return to our metaphor of driving through the fog, she doesn't decide where you should go—she just helps you figure out how to get there. She helps you gather the information you need, evaluate options, consider possibilities, and talk to each other, but she doesn't tell you what to decide.

Sometimes people confuse mediation with arbitration. An arbitrator's role is to hear a dispute and make a decision; the parties decide ahead of time whether that decision will be binding. A mediator, on the other hand, decides nothing other than the procedure for the mediation. She may coax, cajole, reason with, question, share stories and experiences, listen, and sympathize, but she cannot make decisions on legal matters.

Generates Options

Because your mediator has encountered situations similar to yours many times before and is not caught up in the emotional turbulence of your divorce, she's able to think of alternatives you haven't considered—often a great help in breaking impasses.

For example, Becky and George couldn't agree on who should have the right to make decisions about their children's extracurricular activities. Both feared that one would enroll their kids in activities the other would have to pay for or drive them to, yet neither one wanted to obtain the other's approval before making such decisions. So I suggested this: each could enroll the children without the other's approval, so long as that parent paid all of the expense and took the child to all the activities. They liked that solution.

Although this remedy may seem obvious to anyone outside the dispute, such a compromise is often invisible to people caught up in the strong emotions surrounding divorce.

Analyzes Proposals

Many clients bring to mediation agreements reached on their own. Sometimes these settlements are feasible; sometimes they're not. Because of his experience, the mediator may see difficulties in your agreement that you've missed. For example, many couples don't think of the tax implications of their proposals and aren't familiar with the ways they can divide and transfer assets.

At our first meeting, one couple told me that they'd agreed to remain joint owners of their house. The wife would live there, and the husband would receive his share of the equity when it sold years later. I pointed out that they would then need to decide whether they should base his share on the house's present or future value, who would pay for maintenance and repairs, and other issues of joint ownership. When they quickly became entangled in disagreements, I asked why they wanted to stay joint owners. As it turned out, they didn't realize they could transfer ownership of the house to the wife and give the husband something else of comparable value. They quickly agreed to do so.

So if you come to mediation with an agreement, encourage your mediator to help you carefully think it through.

Shares Legal Knowledge

Sometimes a couple will announce that they've agreed to joint custody of their children without realizing what that term means. Or they tell me that they've agreed to a property division when it's clear that they don't understand their legal rights. My job then is to explain what legal terms such as *joint custody* really mean and to be sure they understand that they might be legally entitled to more property, support, or time with their children. They don't have to insist on all of their legal rights, but they shouldn't agree without knowing what those rights are.

How much information the mediator provides depends on how he defines his role and whether he's an attorney. As I discuss in the next chapter, some mediators are not comfortable providing this kind of information to their clients, preferring that the clients rely on their own attorneys for legal information.

The mediator may also raise questions about legal issues the couple hasn't considered. Who gets the tax dependency exemptions for the children? Who will carry the children's medical insurance and pay for uninsured medical expenses? If one person is to pay the other money, when and how will that be done? Will that debt be secured by property?

Offers Evaluations

Sometimes spouses who disagree on an issue ask the mediator how he thinks a court would decide it. In effect, the couple is asking the mediator to provide an evaluation. If he's an experienced family law attorney, his opinion may be valuable in helping each party decide when to take a stand and when not to.

If you want this kind of help but don't want your spouse to hear the mediator's answer, you may ask to "caucus," that is, meet privately with the mediator. But first be sure that he'll keep the discussion confidential. Not all mediators will, believing that both parties should be privy to all communications.

Prepares Documents

If your mediator is a lawyer, he may prepare some or all of your legal paperwork. If he's not an attorney, he'll instead write up a detailed description of your agreement so that a lawyer may prepare the formal court documents.

Some mediators believe that the mediator, even if he is an attorney, should not draft legal paperwork because doing so might violate his neutrality. I disagree. The mediator is merely translating the couple's agreement into legal form, and the parties' lawyers can review the documents to eliminate any possible bias of the mediator.

Your state, however, may have legal or ethical constraints as to how much document preparation a mediator—even an attorney-mediator—is allowed to do. Ask prospective mediators about any limitations regarding their ability to draft your agreement.

Guides You Through the Legal Process

Your mediator's role is to guide you toward settlement. She helps you gather all the information you need to make informed decisions, keeps you on track as she leads you through the legal issues, suggests options you may not have thought of, minimizes unproductive discussions, and keeps you mindful of your best interests and those of your children.

She prods, nudges, asks questions, clarifies your concerns, organizes your discussions, and keeps you talking to each other in a way that leads to agreement and settlement.

Because she cannot give legal advice, your mediator will also be urging you to meet with your own, independent counsel. In the next chapter, we'll consider the importance of getting outside advice, how to make the most of it, and how to keep it from destroying your agreements.

5

Conferring with a Family Law Attorney

When I recommend that clients meet with their own attorneys during mediation, I often see their backs go up. "That's why we're mediating," they explain. "We want to avoid lawyers. They'll just charge a lot of money and get us fighting with each other!"

Having warned you of the dangers of litigation and the traditional adversarial contest, why am I now urging you to see attorneys? Because lawyers have other skills to offer—as advisers and drafters of documents—and you need those skills in mediation. Moreover, you can take advantage of them for a modest cost and without being drawn into battle.

What can a lawyer do that your mediator cannot? Your mediator's job is to help you and your spouse reach an agreement, but because he is neutral, he cannot advise you as to whether your agreement is wise. Remember that, in driving through the fog, *you* choose your destination; your mediator merely helps you get there.

Your lawyer, on the other hand, helps you think clearly about your destination. She's concerned about your needs; she's there to look after your interests—by advising, coaching, and commiserating. You don't have to take her advice, but her knowledge of the complicated world you've just entered and her focus on your welfare make her a valuable resource.

So—unless you have no children and very little property—you both should visit, at least briefly, with separate attorneys who will help you understand what a reasonable agreement might look like.

Clients often ask if they both can use the same lawyer. No. You're seeing a lawyer to help you think about and decide what's best for you, but what's best for you may not be the same as what's best for your spouse. Because you may have conflicting interests, one lawyer cannot advise you both. Ethical guidelines prohibit attorneys from advising opposing parties in litigation—which you and your spouse are.

But seeing two lawyers does not mean ending up in a fight. Later I'll describe how to make use of their legal knowledge without going to war or significantly increasing your expenses.

Why You Need Legal Advice

Divorce is a major legal event in your life. It would be foolish to make important decisions about your future and that of your children without first being sure you understand your legal rights and the legal ramifications of any agreements you make. You probably wouldn't enter any other important contractual agreement, such as a business contract, without legal advice; use that same good sense in handling your divorce.

Some clients expect a mediator to fill them in on legal matters, and to some extent he may. But as I've said, because he must remain neutral, he can't give legal advice; how he defines "advice" will determine how much he can tell you. Thus it's best to meet with an attorney of your own for legal guidance.

Clients sometimes hesitate to get legal advice for fear of angering their spouses. I'd be very suspicious of a spouse who didn't want me to consult a lawyer. Seeing one doesn't mean you're preparing for battle; it means you want to understand how the law applies to your divorce. Considering that you can't knowledgeably discuss the legal issues that arise in mediation without such information, this is not the time to placate your spouse.

You'll probably want to meet with your attorney before mediation to be sure you understand your rights. You may also want to see him occasionally during mediation to discuss legal issues that arise, options, and strategies. He can also review legal papers drafted by the mediator to ensure that your agreement is properly stated and that you understand all of its implications. If your mediator is not an attorney, you'll need a lawyer to draft your legal documents.

How much will this cost? Your consultations need not be expensive. If you call an attorney and ask him to represent you, he'll probably quote a retainer of several thousand dollars. But if you tell him you're mediating your divorce and simply need to consult with him, he should charge by the hour, and you may need no more than an hour or two of his time.

Because most experienced family law attorneys charge between $100 and $300 an hour (depending on the size of your city and the attorney's years of experience), you may each spend no more than $100 to $200 for this advice. If your divorce is very simple, you may pay less; if it's very complicated, you may pay more.

Even with the addition of your attorneys' fees, the total cost of mediation is still considerably lower than the alternative.

What a Consulting Attorney Does

Your consulting attorney has many roles: teacher, coach, friend, and teammate.

Educates You About Your Legal Rights

Your lawyer's job is *not* to insist that you fight for every possible legal advantage but to make sure you understand your legal rights so that you can make informed decisions. Her task is to explain your rights according to state law and local practice and to tell you what you could expect if your divorce were tried in court. You can't make intelligent decisions in mediation without such advice.

Advises You

Your lawyer will also recommend what you should or shouldn't agree to, based on her understanding of your legal rights. You may or may not decide to follow her recommendations, but you certainly want to hear them.

It's true that some lawyers are so oriented toward litigation that they may encourage you to adopt an adversarial stance even when you've made it plain that you don't wish to. You can, however, avoid those lawyers geared for courtroom battles. Later in this chapter I discuss methods for finding a good consulting family lawyer and give you tips for avoiding those who would draw you into combat.

Supports Your Position

If you want to take a firm stand in mediation but are inexperienced at negotiations or have difficulty holding your own with your spouse, you'll welcome your attorney's support and encouragement. She'll be your coach—suggesting options and approaches, strengthening your resolve, affirming your legal rights, and generally helping you be strong.

Strategizes

If your divorce becomes intensely negotiated, your lawyer can suggest strategies. Negotiating is what lawyers spend much of their time doing, so her experience in this area may be very helpful. She can suggest what offers you might make, when to say yes, and when to say no.

A good consulting attorney can be invaluable. She's your counselor and supporter. Use her advice to educate yourself; then make your own decisions.

What Qualifications Your Attorney Should Have

Find a consulting attorney who's knowledgeable about family law and who understands and is sympathetic to mediation.

Get a Knowledgeable Family Law Attorney

Sometimes a client tells me that he's discussed his divorce with his cousin who's a lawyer or that he consulted with his business attorney. Although relatives and business acquaintances may be cheaper and more convenient, they're not going to do you much good unless they're knowledgeable and experienced in family law. It's rather like asking an internist to perform brain surgery.

In the last few years, family law has become so complicated that most lawyers who work in this field don't extend their practices much beyond it. Keeping up with recent court decisions and statutory changes in family law is not something one can do well while focusing one's professional attention elsewhere. Therefore you probably don't want a lawyer who practices "a little" family law. That lawyer may not be knowledgeable about recent developments in the law and how judges in your area are deciding issues.

Many family law attorneys occasionally handle other matters, such as wills and probate, but look for one who practices at least 50 percent family law.

There are exceptions to this rule. If an attorney in your area has an excellent reputation for handling family law matters and has done so for many years, even though it's not his specialty, you may still want to consider him. Or if you live in a smaller community where lawyers cannot concentrate in one area of law, then look for one who regularly handles divorces.

Get a Lawyer Who Believes in Mediation

All lawyers now practicing have been educated in litigation, and many are uncomfortable in other formats. Some may believe that your rights can be protected only by an adversarial process, and they have difficulty working with a client who doesn't think likewise.

Clients often assume that lawyers who favor litigation are simply trying to generate fees, and no doubt that motivation sometimes enters the picture. But many lawyers truly believe that litigation is the best way to protect the legal rights of both parties and that mediation, especially without the parties' lawyers present, is dangerous and inadvisable. Therefore, if you intend to mediate your divorce without the presence of your legal counsel, avoid choosing a litigation-oriented attorney.

How to Find Your Consulting Attorney

If you've already contacted your mediator, ask him to recommend a consulting attorney. He can probably give you and your spouse the names of lawyers experienced at working with mediation clients.

If you don't yet have a mediator or he isn't comfortable giving referrals, try other sources, such as your county bar association's lawyer referral service, friends who've been through divorce, the Web, and the Yellow Pages. If you know lawyers who practice in other legal areas, ask them for referrals.

If, however, your referral source doesn't know the lawyer's qualifications and attitude toward mediation, find out by asking the lawyer such questions as the following:

- How much of your practice is family law, and how long have you been practicing in that area? (At least 50 percent and five years of experience would be best.)

- How do you feel about mediation, especially when attorneys aren't present?

- Have you consulted with other clients who mediated their divorce without their lawyers present? How many? Were you comfortable in that role?

- Would you be comfortable advising me even if I choose not to insist on all my legal rights?

- Would you be comfortable helping me devise unorthodox arrangements for the care of my children if my spouse and I agree on them?

- What is your hourly rate?

Listen carefully to the tone of the response. If an attorney ex-presses exasperation or impatience, he may distrust the mediation process.

Most lawyers will talk to you about such issues before you come in. They probably won't want to give you legal advice over the phone—after all, that is what they get paid for—but they'll usually discuss their qualifications in a preliminary telephone conversation.

If a potential attorney doesn't return your call within twenty-four hours, you'll probably want to move on. Working with an at-torney who doesn't respond readily to client calls can be frustrating.

What to Discuss with Your Attorney

To use your lawyer's time (and fee) effectively, think carefully about what help you want from her—before you get to her office.

Clarifying Her Role

Your attorney is a valuable source of information, advice, ideas, and support. But before tapping this help, be sure you're clear with her about her role. Tell her you believe in and are (or will be) engaged in mediation. Then explain what you want from her, such as infor-mation about your legal rights, help in getting information from your spouse, advice on how to respond to offers from your spouse, and an opinion as to whether your agreement sounds reasonable.

You'll also want to let her know that although you value her ad-vice, you expect to decide for yourself what's best for you and your family and may not choose to take some of her recommendations. Tell her you'll want to talk over your decisions with her to ensure you understand their legal implications, but that you expect her to respect your independence.

If your attorney has trouble accepting the role of consultant rather than warrior, consider changing lawyers.

Educating You About Your Rights

Once you've clarified the kind of help you want, take advantage of all your lawyer's knowledge and experience.

State law determines your rights regarding children, property, and spousal support. As a mediator I discuss broadly the issues you'll be deciding, but only a family law attorney in your state can tell you how the state defines your legal rights. Before beginning mediation, carefully question your lawyer about these issues to be sure you're clear about your rights.

Gathering Information

If you don't know much about your assets and debts, ask your lawyer how to gather this information. Because you're planning to mediate your divorce, you probably don't want her to gather it for you but rather to advise you about what to ask for. Thus you'll go to mediation with a list of the documents and information you need to make educated decisions.

If your spouse refuses to provide necessary information or documents, then ask your lawyer to initiate "formal discovery," whereby she sends your spouse or his attorney a formal request for materials. Your spouse must comply with discovery requests as long as they're reasonable.

Reviewing the Final Paperwork

When your final papers are drafted, bring them to your lawyer to review. These documents are usually very long and detailed, and your mediator will probably welcome having them scrutinized by your attorney. Everyone makes mistakes—but the more people there are to examine the documents, the less likely that errors will go undetected. By checking the clarity of the language in your agreement, your lawyer may help you avoid returning to court or mediation to clarify or enforce your rights.

The mediator and the parties' lawyers can work amicably to complete the legal paperwork. This process need not be antagonistic; it's simply an opportunity to use all the knowledge and experience available.

When Not to Listen

If your attorney is uncomfortable in his role as consultant and isn't able to adjust to it, be careful that he doesn't pull you out of mediation and into litigation.

I once sent a couple to confer with their lawyers in the middle of mediation, not because we'd reached an impasse but because they were fighting hard over inconsequential matters. I thought that their lawyers, by clarifying their legal rights on the contested issues, would encourage them to compromise.

I was wrong. The lawyers made it worse. The attorneys were soon arguing with each other even more than the clients had been, and the parties never returned to mediation.

I'm not telling you this story to scare you away from consulting a lawyer. As I have said, your consulting attorney is a valuable resource for you, but you may have to monitor his participation to be sure that you don't lose control of your case.

At some point, your lawyer may conclude that mediation has failed and recommend litigation. Don't act on his advice without checking with your mediator to see if she too believes mediation is truly at an end. Your lawyer may have reached a premature decision.

Part II

The Process of Mediation

6

Before the First Session

I think mediation is a good idea," the voice on the other end of the phone tells me, "but I'm not sure my wife will agree. What can I say to convince her?"

Another caller explains, "We've decided to mediate and are calling to make an appointment. Is there anything we can do to prepare?"

This chapter answers these questions. It tells you how to talk to your spouse about mediation and how to prepare so that your time there is more productive.

Talking to Your Spouse About Mediation

As I have mentioned elsewhere, it's a good idea to discuss mediation before either of you retains an attorney. Many clients call me after they've hired lawyers and spent a great deal more money than they needed to. Lonny and Regina came in to see me after such an experience. Lonny recounted what had happened.

"I told my lawyer that Regina and I were pretty much in agreement about everything, that we didn't want to fight and I didn't see any reason to. We just needed a lawyer to draft the paperwork."

Regina piped in. "But then I got served with a temporary restraining order. Lonny said he didn't know anything about it, but a hearing was set for a week later, and I was terrified. Our lawyers started fighting, and both of us were paying thousands of dollars for work we didn't want. How did this happen?"

Sometimes lawyers initiate a battle the clients didn't ask for, as happened to Lonny and Regina. Sometimes a client allows or even encourages an attorney to take an aggressive stance because the client is angry. Other clients are simply unaware of alternatives. Regardless of the reason, if damage is done at the beginning of the divorce, it may be hard to undo.

Therefore I suggest you try to interest your spouse in mediation before you contact lawyers. Make it clear that you expect both of you to consult attorneys, but with the understanding that you'll be mediating your divorce.

What to Say to Your Spouse

In approaching your spouse about mediation, you might make the following points:

* *It's a lot less expensive.* Mediated divorces are usually a fraction of the cost of litigated divorces. Your spouse need only discuss litigation fees with a few family law attorneys to understand that the traditional approach to divorce is costly. If you've already contacted a mediator and have received an estimate of her fee, share that information with your spouse so he can compare costs.

* *It's less damaging to your children.* You both have probably known couples who have litigated their divorces and ended up in horrible fights that were hard on their families. Children torn between warring parents end up scarred and miserable. Mediation prevents such casualties among the innocent.

* *It offers an opportunity to end your marriage with your mutual respect and dignity intact.* Assure your spouse that you want to retain your mutual goodwill and that mediation will help you do so. A lit-

igated divorce can destroy your positive feelings and leave you enemies, sore with hurt and hostility.

Warning: this does not mean saying, "You'd better do this or I'll
be really mad and make your life miserable." That is a threat, not
an invitation. You want to encourage your spouse to try an approach
that won't force you to become enemies.

- *It allows you to make your own decisions about the future care of
your children and the division of your estate, instead of turning those decisions over to lawyers and judges.* The adversarial nature of litigation
makes it difficult if not impossible to create imaginative solutions
that meet the unique needs of your family. If a judge makes the decisions for you, she will probably apply state guidelines—boilerplate
provisions that may not suit you, your spouse, or your children.

Mediation gives you the freedom to create arrangements that
specifically fit your family, allowing you to answer such questions as:
Who has the children when? How will we make decisions about
their care? How should we divide our property? How can we meet
everyone's future economic needs? Mediation allows you to avoid
being forced into a standardized framework devised by the state.

- *It's private.* All documents filed in a litigated divorce and
every statement made in court are part of the public record. In most
cases, anyone can sit in the courtroom and listen to you, your attorneys, and witnesses discuss intimate family matters. In mediation, probably no one but you, your spouse, and your mediator are
in her office, and most states don't allow statements made there to
be repeated in court.

You might introduce mediation to your spouse by sharing this
book. Or ask your mediator if she has literature on mediation that
you and your spouse can read and discuss.

Discussing Possible Agreements

The more you and your spouse agree on *before* mediation, the easier and less expensive it'll be. Once you've agreed to mediate and have conferred with your attorneys, sit down together to see how many issues you can resolve on your own.

I know that some couples are too angry to talk this way and will only make matters worse by trying. If that's your situation, don't be discouraged. Mediators are trained to get you to participate in productive discussions, even when the two of you can hardly bear to be in the same room. Indeed, those couples who *cannot* stand being together are usually separated during the first session. If this is the case with you and your spouse, tell the mediator ahead of time so she can plan to separate you.

Fortunately, most couples can discuss their children and property before mediation and reach some agreements. Some even come to mediation with most issues resolved; they need me primarily to prepare their legal paperwork.

If you and your spouse can discuss the issues that you'll be deciding in mediation, write down what you agree on—you can give this list to your mediator. If you quarrel over any issue, put it aside for mediation. The following are some guidelines for your discussion.

Your Future Economic Pictures

Each of you might begin by filling out Appendix Two, the income and expense form, and comparing the results. Seeing each other's future income and expenses helps promote mutual understanding and empathy. Moreover, this information is essential when you discuss child support, property division, and spousal support.

Who Will Have the Children When

It's worth discussing this, for you may find that you have similar ideas. While exploring possibilities, keep in mind everyone's schedules and the importance of your children maintaining a good relationship with both parents in a stable environment. Don't worry about who has "custody" (an ambiguous term with powerful emotional overtones) or about how spending time with your children might affect child support.

Custody

This topic is so legally complex that it's better to discuss it with a knowledgeable mediator who can guide you through the issues involved.

Child Support

If you both have discussed state guidelines with your attorneys and feel comfortable applying them to your situation—keeping in mind what you need and can afford—then try agreeing on an amount of child support. But don't make firm agreements on this or anything else until you understand your legal rights.

Inventory of Property and Debts

Work together to fill in Appendix One, the property chart. List all property and debts and gather all the information you need to assign specific values and amounts for each. Of course, if your estate is very simple and you both agree on who gets what, you may not need to go through this exercise. But most couples aren't sure what's fair until they see the numbers in black and white.

When you have listed all the assets and debts (with their values), you can consider how to divide them, after first deciding what percentage goes to each of you. Your lawyers should be able to tell you what portion of the estate each of you would probably receive under your state law.

If you see a number of options for dividing your estate, discuss these with your lawyers or mediator, who will help you evaluate them.

Spousal Support

Reviewing your income and expense forms and talking to your attorneys should prepare you to discuss possible alimony payments: how much and for how long. The two of you may be able to make some of these decisions before mediation.

Making an Appointment

Having discussed the issues reviewed in this chapter, having learned about your legal rights, and having explored tentative agreements, you can begin mediation.

Before making an appointment, be sure your spouse understands and has agreed to mediation and that the time is convenient. I've had mediations start on the wrong foot when these amenities were not honored; for example, one client grumbled, "My wife told me to be here at two o'clock. I don't know what this is about."

I usually suggest that the caller give her spouse my name and phone number so that he can call me to ask questions and to discuss mediation with him. That way mediation is clearly a mutual decision and not something one spouse is dragging the other to.

Make an Appointment for Both of You

Sometimes a client asks to come to the first appointment alone. Although your mediator may have a different viewpoint, I recommend that you come in together for your first session. As I said earlier, if I meet with one spouse first, the other may see me as biased, an advocate for the first spouse. Once that happens, my effectiveness as a mediator is eroded.

A client sometimes asks if I'll call the other spouse to talk about mediation. I decline. I don't feel it's appropriate for me to try talking someone into using my services; the caller should do the persuading. However, I know that some mediators are more comfortable promoting their services, so you might ask your mediator if she's willing to talk to your spouse about coming in.

Pre-Mediation Conversations

Can you discuss your situation on the phone with a mediator before coming in? I see no harm in doing so. If you want to fill her in on some background, she'll probably listen and possibly take notes. Experienced mediators are not likely to be biased by these communications, because they've learned that there are two sides to every story.

However, having a conversation with the mediator about the details of your divorce before your first visit may be a waste of time. The mediator talks to many people over the phone; some become clients and some don't. She may not take notes or remember anything you told her, making it necessary to repeat everything later. If it's important to you to communicate certain information about your situation to the mediator ahead of time and you want her to remember it, tell her so, so she'll take notes.

In a recent telephone conversation with me, a woman described an issue she and her husband needed to mediate in their divorce; she then said she thought it best that they do nothing on the matter until they came in a few days later.

"What do you think about my inclination to wait?" she asked. "Sounds like a reasonable approach," I responded.

The husband called me later that day saying, "My wife says you advised her that we should do nothing until we see you. Is that right?"

If you do discuss matters with the mediator ahead of time, do not use the mediator's comments as a weapon against your spouse. Such a tactic will make your spouse distrust the mediator, thereby diminishing—if not destroying—the effectiveness of mediation.

Appointments Set by Your Lawyers

If you plan to come to mediation with your attorneys, they'll probably make the appointment and discuss your case ahead of time with the mediator. Usually the lawyers send the mediator a written analysis of the issues, and the mediator may then call them to discuss the case in more detail. These discussions are confidential. Each side is encouraged to be open and frank about the case, knowing that nothing said will be repeated to the other side. The more the mediator knows, the better prepared she is to help you settle your case.

What to Take with You to Mediation

Clients often ask what to bring to their first session. If your mediator is a family law attorney and will be drafting your legal paperwork, bring him the documents and information listed in the following section; if your consulting attorney will draft the legal instruments, then she's the one who should receive this material. (In Chapter Seven I discuss the relative merits of having your mediator or your consulting attorney draft legal documents.)

The following documents will probably be needed to draft your legal paperwork; bringing them to your first mediation session may save you time later.

1.   *Real estate documents.* If either of you owns a home or other real property, bring a document that gives a legal description of the property and any notes secured by it. In my home state, the deed of trust provides that information; in your area it may be called something else. If you aren't sure, bring all documents you received at closing; the mediator can choose what he needs. If you've refinanced the property, bring the documents from that transaction.

2.   *Vehicle identification numbers.* If you'll be transferring title to any of your vehicles, bring their vehicle identification numbers with you.

3. *Retirement account information.* If you think you may divide your retirement benefits or those of your spouse, bring the most current statement of the account and the booklet that explains the plan and its benefits. If your employer has developed a model QDRO (see Chapter Fourteen, "Dividing It All Up," for a discussion of QDROs), bring that as well.

4. *Social Security and driver's license numbers.* Bring these numbers for yourself, your spouse, and your children.

5. *Debt information.* For any debts that you don't pay off monthly, bring the name of the creditor, the account number, and the balance owing. This includes credit cards, student loans, vehicle loans, and personal loans.

6. *Inventory.* It's helpful to the mediator to have an inventory of your assets and debts, perhaps in the form shown in Appendix One. Your inventory can also show how you propose to divide up assets and debts, if you're ready to make a proposal.

If you and your spouse worked together preparing the inventory and agree on values and any part of the division of property and debts, all the better. This inventory can save the mediator a good deal of time in understanding your estate.

If it's going to take a lot of time to gather all these documents, you needn't delay your mediation while you do so. You can always bring the documents in later. And the mediator may request additional documents when she knows more about your estate and how you plan to divide it.

———————

You're now ready to begin mediation; in the next chapter I describe what to expect at your first meeting.

7

The First Session
(and What Happens Next)

T his was a lot easier than I thought it would be!" That's the comment I hear most often from clients at the end of their first session.

Clients are often tense when we begin. They've dreaded talking to a lawyer about the details of their divorce, stirring up their hurt and anger—the prospect is scary.

During this first session, though, the ice is broken. As we address the practical details, clients soon realize that divorce is not the nightmare they envisioned but a manageable process; they can talk to each other and make sensible decisions.

Although mediators vary in their methodology, I doubt that your experience will differ greatly from the process in my office, so I'll describe our procedure to give you an idea of what to expect.

These are the steps we begin at our first meeting:

- Understanding the rules of mediation

- Clarifying your goals in the divorce

- Tackling the legal issues

- Initiating the legal paperwork

- Preparing the final orders

- Finalizing your divorce

When clients are fairly agreeable and their estate is relatively simple, they resolve all their issues in their first session—which rarely exceeds two to three hours.

Sometimes, however, couples need additional meetings to address all their concerns. We may discuss the children at our first session and consider property issues later. Occasionally clients need to come in three or four times, but rarely more.

Understanding the Rules

One reason the mediator succeeds in helping you reach an agreement is that she has rules—both for mediation and for her services. These rules are designed to keep the mediation from disintegrating into arguments, to protect your privacy, and to clarify her role and her fee. She will probably provide you a copy of the rules and review them with you.

Rules for Mediation

I ask clients to read the rules for mediation (reproduced in Appendix Three) before we begin. You might look those over now too. Your mediator may have a somewhat different set of rules, but they'll probably be quite similar.

These rules ensure that everyone has his say, uninterrupted; that everyone is treated with respect; and that no one's rights are prejudiced in mediation.

Employment Contract

I ask clients to read my employment contract before we meet. It states not only my hourly rate but also that I'm a neutral intermediary who represents neither party and that they should consult their own attorneys instead of relying on me for legal advice. Before we begin, I want to be sure my clients are clear about my role and the importance of obtaining independent legal counsel.

We review this agreement at the end of our first session, and I give them a signed copy.

Clarifying Your Goals

Your mediator will probably begin the first session by restating some of the points in the rules. He may then complete the employment contract with you or wait until the end of your session to do so.

After attending to these preliminary matters, he'll invite you both to share information about your children, property, and other relevant matters. I ask clients whether and when they separated and if they think I need to know anything else about their marital history before we begin. Some clients shake their heads no, and we jump into the legal issues regarding their children. Others tell me about events leading up to their divorce. I leave it to my clients to decide how much marital background they wish to share.

This is a good time to talk about your goals in mediation. One client, Claire, did so by telling me that she and Bob still cared for each other and wanted to end their marriage as friends. "We have two kids, and we don't want to end up like some of our friends, bickering for years and dragging our children through all that muck." Glancing nervously at Bob, she added, "I'm concerned though about my income after the divorce. Bob makes a lot more than I do, and I don't want to slide into poverty because of this."

Another client, Mike, said he wanted to avoid lawyers and fighting. He was also worried about money. "We've got a ton of bills, which I guess I'll have to pay, but Mary's telling me she wants alimony too, and I don't see how I can do both. She wants to keep the house, and that means I'm going to need enough money to buy another one." Looking sheepishly at me, he ended, "We're hoping you can help us figure out how to do all this."

Tackling the Legal Issues

Your mediator will introduce you to the legal landscape, explaining terms and pointing out issues that you'll need to address regarding your children and property. Some of these issues will be familiar and perhaps already agreed on; others will be new points you haven't considered.

If the two of you have filled out an inventory like that in Appendix One or have reached tentative agreements, share these with your mediator. Ted and Marcy began by showing me a property chart they'd worked out.

"We figure the equity in the house is about equal to the value of Ted's 401K, and both are subject to tax," Marcy explained. "So we've agreed that Ted'll keep his retirement and I'll keep the house. And we can divide everything else up evenly."

As she paused, Ted added, "What we're having trouble with is child support. We've agreed the kids will spend alternating weeks with each of us, and we think we want joint custody, but we aren't sure what that means. Maybe you can explain it to us."

Marcy continued. "Ted doesn't think he should pay child support, but he makes twice what I do. I think he should help me out with expenses. So we haven't resolved that one," she finished, smiling warily at Ted.

Providing this kind of overview—what you've agreed on and where your difficulties lie—gives your mediator a quick outline with which to work. She will, of course, review your agreements in some detail to be sure she understands them and that you've thought through all the implications.

If you and your spouse have agreed on nothing and don't know where to begin, that's OK. Many clients begin mediation with no agreements and little understanding of the issues before them.

Initiating the Legal Paperwork

If your mediator is going to draft your legal paperwork, she may prepare your initial pleadings following your first session. These documents officially begin the divorce proceedings and start the clock ticking at the courthouse. Most states require minimum waiting periods from the time you file pleadings until the divorce can be finalized. The length of that period varies from state to state; in Texas, for example, it's sixty days.

Your mediator can't sign these documents as your attorney of record; rather, you'll sign them yourselves. In doing so, you'll be "pro se" or "pro per," that is, representing yourselves rather than being represented by counsel. You can, if you prefer, ask one of your lawyers to draft and file the pleadings.

The mediator or your attorney will file these papers at the courthouse to initiate the divorce action, and you'll pay a filing fee to the county. The amount varies; in my county it's about $165.

Preparing the Final Orders

Your legal documents may be simple or complex, depending on the complexity of your estate and your agreement and on the requirements of state law. It's imperative that these documents be properly prepared to ensure that your agreement is clear and legally binding on you both.

Who Should Prepare the Paperwork?

As the two of you reach agreements, the mediator will reduce them to writing. If he's a family law attorney and you've designated him to prepare your documents, he'll write up your agreement in the form required by the court. Otherwise, he'll summarize your agreement for the lawyer who will prepare the legal documents.

In most cases it's more efficient for the mediator to prepare the orders rather than summarize the agreement for another attorney. For one thing, because he's participating in the discussions, he has a clear understanding of your decisions. If he merely summarizes your agreement, it may take a good deal of time for him to write up that summary and even more time for a lawyer to translate it into legalese. And because that lawyer didn't attend your session, she may lose something in the translation. If that happens, you, the mediator, and the drafting attorney must communicate further to iron out the problems.

If one spouse's lawyer writes up the final orders, the other spouse may distrust her neutrality. I've seen my clients' lawyers haggle over details, both suspecting the other of trying to gain an advantage. When the mediator prepares the orders, his clients and their attorneys usually assume the documents are free of bias.

If your mediator is not an attorney, then you must ask your or your spouse's lawyer to prepare the final orders, unless the mediator works with a neutral attorney. Therapist-mediators occasionally arrange to have a neutral attorney attend the final mediation session to take notes on all the details of the agreement. That lawyer can then write up the final orders. This is an excellent way to benefit from the joint expertise of a therapist and a lawyer, though it's somewhat more expensive.

When the Final Orders Are Prepared

When my clients agree on all the issues at their first session, I write up their final orders immediately afterward for them to review with their attorneys. When clients agree on only some issues, I may draft a partial order for them to look over before our next session. We can begin the second session by discussing that draft and making any necessary revisions.

Transferring Property

Whoever prepares your final orders will probably prepare documents transferring the title of property—your house, vehicles, retirement benefits, and so on. Because these documents can be very complicated, you'll want to review them, as well as your final orders, with your attorney.

Finalizing Your Divorce

Because most couples want to complete their divorce as soon as possible, we look at our calendars to see how soon we can do that. As the law in our state requires a sixty-day waiting period, we choose a date soon after that period has passed.

You aren't required to complete your divorce as soon as the waiting period has elapsed; you can take as long as you wish, at least in my county. Local practice in your area may be different though, so if you want to take your time completing your divorce, ask your attorney about any time constraints.

Also, some states require divorcing parties to appear in court when the judge signs the final orders; others don't—the mediator or attorney can simply mail them to court for the judge's signature.

In the next three chapters I'll discuss the tactical and emotional issues in mediation—how the mediator guides you toward an agreement and how you can help by successfully navigating the emotional hurdles.

8

How Agreements Are Reached

Max and Beverly had decided to divorce, but they couldn't work out their finances.

"Look," began Max, "I can give you $650 a month for the kids. That's more than enough to cover my share of their expenses, and there's no way I can pay any more. I'll barely be making it as it is."

"Six hundred and fifty dollars! That won't even pay child care!" Beverly snapped. "And I'll need help with the house payment too. I can't afford $1,200 a month on my salary."

"You think you're going to stay in the house?" Max was incredulous. "That's ridiculous! We've got to sell the house. Then we both can find something cheaper."

Glaring at her husband, Beverly could barely control her anger. "Oh, great! You're not only leaving me and the kids for your new girlfriend, you're going to force us onto the street! Don't you think these kids have been through enough without having to lose their home and friends?"

"Yeah, right, this is all my fault, as usual!" Max flung back as he slammed the front door behind him.

If you and your spouse end up shouting when you talk about your divorce, why is it going to be any different in mediation? It'll be different because your mediator has the rules and skills to channel your discussions into productive problem solving. With his help, you'll be focusing on your legal issues, gathering relevant information, considering your options, and making mutual decisions with which both of you can live. In this chapter, I'll give you a clearer picture of how that process works.

Identifying the Issues

The mediator will first lead you through the issues regarding your children and property, alimony, and taxes. On some points, you and your spouse already agree or will do so quickly, but on others you'll need to give careful thought. The mediator will be listening for the knotty issues, knowing that you'll be concentrating on those in mediation. One couple may disagree on the amount of child support; another may focus on how long alimony should last or who gets the house.

Tom and Suzie, a couple in their early forties, were most concerned about Tom's retirement benefits and their debts. As we reviewed their property, they knew which car each would keep and that Suzie would stay in the house with the children. But when I asked about their retirement benefits, Tom bristled.

"I've worked hard for ten years to accumulate those benefits. They're mine," Tom declared. "Suzie has her own retirement. She can keep hers and I'll keep mine."

Suzie looked uncomfortable. "Tom doesn't want to give me any of his retirement, and that's OK with me if that's what's fair." Glancing at Tom she added, "What I'm concerned about are our debts. I can't pay off our credit cards on my salary." For them to decide what was "fair" and who would pay off the debts, we needed more information.

Gathering Information

You can't know if an agreement is reasonable without knowing all the facts: the value of each asset, the amount of each debt, your financial needs after divorce, your rights under state law, and every-thing else that bears on the issues to be resolved.

If some of the information isn't readily available, the mediator will ask you to gather it before the next session. You may need to obtain the loan balance on the house, the cost of the children's medical insurance, or an estimate of your own expenses after the divorce.

She may give you forms to fill out or recommend experts who can provide necessary advice. For example, you may need to hire an actuary to appraise pension benefits or a CPA to discuss the tax implications of a proposal. And you'll want to confer with your at-torney to be clear about your legal rights.

If your spouse seems to be hiding assets, raise this in mediation and with your attorney. The mediator can ask both spouses to pre-pare sworn inventories, filed with the court, listing all assets and debts with correct values. If you later discover that your spouse's in-ventory was fraudulent, you can claim a share of any undisclosed property.

Your lawyer may also, if necessary, demand the information by sending formal discovery requests—a more expensive alternative that you should use only as a last resort.

One way to begin gathering information about your property is by filling out the blank chart shown in Appendix One. The first chart you see is Tom and Suzie's. There is also a blank form for you to use. (We'll examine Appendix One in more detail in Chapters Thirteen and Fourteen.)

To decide what would happen to Tom's retirement and their credit card debts, we needed more information, so I asked Tom and Suzie to determine the market values of their assets and the bal-ances owing on their debts.

By talking to realtors and consulting a Blue Book, they came up with values for the house and cars that they agreed were reasonable. Their insurance agent told them the present cash surrender values of their whole-life policies, and an actuary helped us evaluate their retirement benefits. A few phone calls gave them the balances on their debts. With that information we filled in the property chart as you see it in Appendix One.

Both also met with their lawyers to understand better how a judge would probably divide their property if they didn't agree.

When Suzie and Tom had completed the property chart, Tom was startled. "I thought that if I took all the credit card debt and gave her the house, she'd be getting a good deal and I'd be a hero. Now it looks like I'm making out like a bandit!"

When all the property information is clearly presented, your idea of a "fair" settlement may change dramatically. Tom and Suzie did work out a reasonable property division, as I describe later, but it looked different from the version they started with.

Considering Options

Some questions have several possible answers. For example, as you can see from Appendix One, Tom and Suzie's house is worth less than the balance owing on their mortgage. (They bought it just before a drop in the real estate market.) Therefore, if they want to split their estate evenly but prefer that Suzie keep the house, they must divide Tom's retirement. But if they decide to sell their home and have each of them absorb half the loss, Tom could keep more of his retirement, more of the cash, and less debt. Or Tom could keep *all* of his retirement if he took the house and the car with the large debt on it.

As you consider your children and your property, spend time generating options. In what ways can you divide, sell, or continue to share your assets and still come out with a fair division? What alternatives can you imagine for sharing the care of your children that give them access to you both?

Your mediator can help by offering options. She's probably seen many situations similar to yours and has considerable experience discussing alternatives.

Once you've laid out every option you can think of, consider the strengths and weaknesses of each. Retaining joint ownership of the house would give Tom the advantage of sharing its negative equity and keeping more of his retirement. On the other hand, he'd stay economically tied to Suzie for years. Would he have to pay part of the mortgage, part of the maintenance? What if the air conditioner went out? For Suzie it meant help with the house expenses but lack of control. For example, she wouldn't be able to sell the house without Tom's agreement.

Making Decisions

Suzie and Tom divided their assets based on the numbers and on their personal values, such as the importance of stability for their children. They agreed that it was better for the kids to remain at home with their mother for several years, and they didn't want the headache of jointly owning the house. They also agreed that Suzie's lower income was insufficient to pay off their credit cards or to obtain financing for a new house. They therefore had to split Tom's retirement benefits evenly.

Working out an agreement regarding your children follows a similar process. Once you've considered everyone's schedules and needs and your goals for your children, a plan is likely to emerge. If your children are small, if stability is most important to you, and if one parent has provided most of their care, then suddenly shifting them between parents on alternating weeks is probably not appropriate. Suppose that Mom's work sends her out of town half the time and that Dad, who has been very involved in the children's care, has an eight-to-five job with almost no travel—Dad may be the better choice for primary caretaker.

Staying on Track

As you work through these decisions, your mediator will keep you on track and not let you get derailed by arguments and irrelevant concerns.

It's easy for the parties to go from one point to another without making decisions. One thing reminds them of another, and they shift the subject again and again, becoming increasingly frustrated by the lack of resolution. Your mediator watches for such blind alleys and will rope you in when she sees you heading down them.

Arguments also lead you into a bog of barren struggle and away from the path of useful decision making. Your mediator will curtail argument when it is shedding no light on the subject.

———————

Using the tools we've discussed, the mediator will guide you toward resolution. But success depends on you and your spouse, and the next two chapters explore the difficulties with which you may wrestle as you work toward agreement.

9

The Emotional Hurdles—What Works

While your mediator is focusing your discussions on the legal decisions that must be made, you and your spouse may be feeling the swirl of emotions attending divorce—anger, fear, bitterness, guilt, distrust, and grief. These emotions can be overwhelming at times and may sabotage your work in mediation if you aren't prepared to check them.

In this chapter, I'll discuss how your good sense, mutual respect, honor, empathy, and restraint can counteract the negative emotions that threaten to swamp you. In the next chapter, we'll look at particular behavior to be avoided.

If you and your spouse have agreed completely on the terms of your divorce or if you're so friendly that you don't expect serious conflicts in mediation, you can skip this chapter and the next.

Most couples, however, find that mediation challenges their ability to remain fair, open minded, and reasonable while discussing emotionally charged issues. So in this chapter we'll review ways to avoid being overwhelmed by the emotional turbulence of divorce:

- Remembering your goal

- Remaining honest and open

- Listening

- Showing respect

- Expressing anger appropriately

- Focusing on the present

- Talking about your needs (not your spouse's failings)

- Taking breaks

- Being reasonable

- Getting the help and support you need

Remembering Your Goal

Your goal, you may be thinking, is to come out of this divorce with as much property, as little debt, and as much time with your children as you can manage. Although you need not abandon those ends, you might temper them with other considerations: fairness, consideration for your spouse, and the best interests of your children.

Walking away with all the winnings may be an empty victory if it means seriously damaging a spouse you once loved. That damage may be to her self-respect, peace of mind, ability to parent well in the future, or financial solvency.

If your success is won at such a price, you're likely to feel soiled rather than satisfied; your spouse is likely to feel resentful; and your children, sensing what's going on around them, may feel confused and betrayed—leaving you with children who resent and distrust you, and with a difficult ex-spouse who undermines your relationship with them.

I often hear a divorcing parent say something like, "I know we'll be dealing with each other for another ten years, when our youngest turns eighteen." I once thought the same thing—that my relationship with my daughter's father ended on her eighteenth birthday. It didn't.

If you have children, your relationship with your spouse will probably continue the rest of your life. Do you want that relationship to be embittered and difficult because you failed to be fair and reasonable in your divorce? Do you want your relationship with your children jeopardized by a resentful ex-spouse?

When you find yourself becoming angry and intransigent in mediation, stop and remember your goals. Break for a few minutes, or a few days. Calm down and reconsider what you want to achieve— a reasonable agreement that recognizes

- Your future needs and those of your spouse and children

- The importance of keeping your spouse's goodwill, particularly if you'll be coparenting

- The importance of keeping your honor and self-esteem intact

Honesty, Empathy, and Responsibility

Robert and Jenny sat at the round table in my office saying nothing. The tension in the air was palpable. Robert was fifty-six, Jenny fifty-five. Married thirty years, they had raised four children while Robert built a successful law practice. Jenny had stayed home with the children, all now successfully launched in their own careers. She had not worked outside the home since she was twenty-five.

During the last two hours, we had reviewed their property and debts. Fortunately, Robert had accumulated a considerable retirement fund, and their home was almost paid for. However, if their assets were divided according to Texas law, Jenny would not have enough to live on.

Robert was well off, for he expected to continue his law practice and he was the only child of wealthy, elderly parents. But Jenny had no job skills and no possibility of inheritance. She could probably earn no more than the minimum wage. And Texas at that time had no alimony statute. A couple could contractually *agree* to spousal support, but a judge could not *order* a spouse to pay alimony after divorce.

Robert wanted this divorce. He'd met another woman—a lawyer in his firm—and was reinvigorated by her youth, energy, and professional success. He felt guilty about leaving Jenny, but he very much wanted this chance for a new beginning.

Jenny was in pain. Although their marriage had become routine and uninspired, it had endured thirty years without major problems. Robert's decision to divorce had not only caught her off guard; it had humiliated and frightened her.

As we examined their assets, Robert stated that he was willing to give Jenny 65 percent of the community estate, a division that their lawyers agreed would be the likely outcome in court. We then reviewed their finances to see what this division would yield each of them after divorce and how each could supplement it with their expected salaries. The results were unsettling. Robert, with his law practice and inheritance, should have no problems; Jenny, on the other hand, saw no way to make ends meet. So there they sat— Robert guilty but determined; Jenny hurt and fearful.

Jenny looked at her husband. "I want alimony, Robert. You know I can't live without something more."

Robert's face tightened. "I'm giving you 65 percent of our estate. Your own lawyer told you that's a generous settlement. My God, when this divorce is over, what I make is mine! I can't keep supporting you!"

Jenny looked like she'd been slapped, but she took a deep breath and continued. "I know our marriage has become stale; I guess I took it for granted. I know too that you want a new start with Meredith." Jenny paused for a moment. "This has all been very painful for me, but you have the right to do what you want. I'm not trying to stop you."

Speaking deliberately and as calmly as she could manage, she continued. "Bob, I'm scared. I've raised four children, kept the house, entertained for you, been available when you needed me. And I have little to show for it. I can't earn $200,000 a year, like you, and I have no parents leaving me money; I can't live on what I can earn. I appreciate your generosity in the property division, but it's simply not enough. I need more."

Jenny fell silent; she waited. The silence hung heavily as Robert fidgeted grimly in his chair. I wondered what was going on behind his impassive expression.

Finally he spoke. "You know, I don't feel good about this. I know it's been hard on you, and I don't want to give you pain. But dammit, Jenny, I really want this new life, and I guess I'm afraid that I'll never be really free." Robert's face had changed: the muscles had relaxed; his eyes were moist. Jenny still said nothing.

"I know you've raised the kids and done all the things you said," he continued. "You've been a good wife and mother. This is not your fault. I just want something else."

Robert, his head down, was staring at his hands on the table. Jenny reached out and touched his arm. "Thanks, Bob," she said softly.

"I know you need more," Robert added, still looking down. "Maybe we could talk about alimony." Raising his eyes to Jenny at last, he explained, "I just want to have my own life."

Robert and Jenny had, with dignity and generosity, acknowledged each other's needs. It was time for me to enter with information about alimony that could help them structure an agreement. They still had many decisions to make: how long alimony would be paid, how much the monthly payments would be, and whether it would end at Jenny's remarriage or at any other event.

These decisions were not easy. Each of them filled out an income and expense form (Appendix Two) at home, and in mediation we discussed the numbers realistically. Both had to continue to listen to the other's concerns and be willing to absorb some pain.

Robert and Jenny eventually reached an agreement that guaranteed Jenny a safe financial future and that Robert felt was fair to both of them; they did it by struggling with their fear and hurt, and calling on the best that was in them.

Successful mediation relies on such courage and character. It also helps *recover* those qualities, often lost in the pain of divorce.

Listening

As Robert and Jenny illustrate, a key tool in reaching a fair settlement is careful listening, a particularly difficult task when one is experiencing the stress of divorce. Robert listened quietly while Jenny spoke, and made it clear that he had heard her. She then waited patiently for him to respond and didn't comment until he'd finished.

Another couple illustrates the mistake of speaking too soon, before you know your spouse's intentions. Jim and Beth were in my office recently, working out the division of a rather large estate. Both were in their late forties. Jim, slender and graying, was an administrator in a government agency. Beth had maintained their home and, with her short red hair and pleasant demeanor, appeared younger than her years.

Beth's inherited property gave her a substantial annual income. Jim earned a good living, but his income was less than Beth's, and he smarted over the difference.

Both had seen lawyers and knew that because state law gave Beth the right to all of her inheritance, she could walk away with most of the property. Although the two had reached a private agreement several weeks before, Beth had recently told Jim that she'd changed her mind. Thus, as they began mediation, Jim was resentful and Beth was wary.

As I asked questions about their property, Jim became increasingly agitated. My attempts to clarify their estate seemed to stir his anger over losing the financial benefits of this marriage; he began accusing Beth of infidelity and threatened to disclose embarrassing personal letters.

Beth maintained her composure during these outbursts, but after several such comments from Jim, she explained with some impatience the division of property she had in mind. The proposal she offered was very generous to her husband, and he quickly accepted it, apologizing for his earlier remarks.

My impression was not that Jim's threats had prompted Beth's generous proposal but rather that they could have precluded it. Jim made the mistake, not fatal in this case, of becoming hostile and belligerent before he knew what his spouse wanted.

Such anger is understandable. By the time you get to mediation, you've experienced a great deal of hurt and disappointment. If, however, you allow such feelings to control your behavior, you may fail to achieve your goals in mediation.

To quell these emotions, force yourself to focus on your spouse's point of view. Ask questions and listen carefully and sympathetically to understand her needs, goals, and feelings. Doing this can keep you both from drowning in a morass of anger and help you reach a reasonable agreement more quickly.

Listening does not mean agreeing. It means understanding. The purpose of listening is to discover your common ground and avoid incorrect assumptions about your spouse's goals. Jim had assumed that Beth's changing her mind meant that she would try to get as much property as she legally could. He was wrong; that was not her intent. And his anger might have destroyed her goodwill.

You should not, of course, ask questions in a manner that suggests condescension, control, ridicule, or cross-examination. Demanding information from the other is not likely to result in a useful exchange. To understand your spouse's point of view, try such expressions as the following:

"Help me understand what you would like to see happen."

"Could you tell me more about that?"

"I'd like to know more about what you think is important here."

If the mediator thinks either of you is not listening to the other, she may intervene to encourage you, which also gives her an opportunity to rephrase and soften the communication, as in the following exchange.

A wife complains, "I don't see how you expect me to raise Brian on $500 a month," and the husband bristles.

"Well, if you didn't spend so much on fancy clothes, $500 would be plenty."

I step in. "It sounds like Theresa is worried that $500 won't be enough to cover your son's expenses, and Skip thinks Theresa could economize more. Is that right? Then let's look at the child's expenses. Theresa, could you tell us what they are?"

When the remarks are rephrased in this way, it's easier for both parties to hear them. Then we can go on to examine the real issue—is $500 enough to cover the child's expenses?

And remember, when you listen and ask questions, you aren't saying that you'll accede to your spouse's desires or feelings; you want only to understand them so that you're in a better position to forge an agreement.

It's likely that you'll not need to ask many questions. Your spouse will probably be eager to state her thoughts and feelings, or she may be prompted to do so by the mediator. Your job then is to listen without interrupting—*really* listen to understand. You might even repeat to her what you heard in order to be sure you got it right and to let your spouse know you were listening to her.

I'm not suggesting that this task is easy. It's hard for most of us to listen patiently and attentively when someone says things with which we strongly disagree or that we even find hurtful or dishonest. But it will greatly help your progress in mediation if you do so.

When we understand that someone is truly interested in what we're saying, we often drop our defensiveness and feel more kindly toward that person. Just having the chance to express ourselves fully without interruption or criticism is such a relief that we're usually grateful to the person giving us the opportunity.

Thus, when you're listening, be careful *not* to disagree, criticize, or correct. You'll later have a chance to express your own viewpoint, which may be quite different. But when you're focusing on the other's position, you'll defeat your purpose if you make negative remarks. You can nod, say that you understand, ask for clarification, and generally be attentive. When you disagree, keep it to yourself for the time being.

Having the opportunity to express herself freely and fully will put your spouse in a much better frame of mind for continuing discussions. Any anger she brought to mediation will be at least partly dissipated by the satisfaction of being heard. She may then be interested in listening to your thoughts, giving you the chance to fully voice your concerns and ideas.

When it appears that your spouse has finished speaking, you may then state your own goals and proposals by saying something like, "Well, I'm glad to know how you feel about this, and I'll need to think about it some more. I'd like to talk about my own goals too, and I have some somewhat different ideas." With this sort of lead-in, your spouse will probably be open to hearing you. And if she's not, the mediator will help you hold the floor while you state your own concerns.

Asking questions and listening carefully to the answers not only put you and your spouse in a better frame of mind but also give you valuable information. You may discover, as Jim did, that your spouse wants many of the same things you do. Once you know the other's goals, you can design a proposal that gives both of you what you want.

Anger blinds us. When we're enraged and frightened, problems seem insurmountable because our emotions block rational thought. If you're able to check your anger and impatience by being a good listener, you can find answers to problems that in the heat of battle seem overwhelming.

Respect

One reason that attentive listening results in solutions is that it accords respect to the speaker, and mutual respect is essential to reaching a satisfying agreement. When you make disparaging and insulting remarks in anger, you damage your chances of reaching your goal. Remember that the person you're speaking to is someone you once loved and perhaps still do and, if you have children, with whom you'll have a relationship for the rest of your life.

Here are some comments that individuals in mediation have made to show their respect for their spouses:

"Kevin's a good daddy. He really has a good relationship with Brian, and it's important to me that they keep that closeness."

"Mary Beth has raised our kids and done a fine job of it. She's kept a beautiful home, and I've really enjoyed having that. She's made it a lot easier for me to concentrate on my job and support the family."

"Pam managed our investments so well that we've saved a lot more than most couples in our situation."

"Our marriage isn't working out, but we're good friends. Brad has contributed as much to this marriage as I have, if not more, and I don't want to do anything that would hurt him."

You can affirm your spouse's contributions and still be realistic about her limitations. If she's lousy at paying her debts, too protective of the children, or not really interested in parenting, you need to keep these facts in mind when making decisions.

But you've also cherished things about this person. Remind yourself of those good qualities before beginning mediation. Your spouse is likely to have a better attitude too if she's heard you affirm her worth and your appreciation of her contributions.

Healthy Anger

I'm not saying that you shouldn't express anger. If anger is appropriate, it may be expressed and can even be helpful in resolving disputes. After all, it's anger that makes us reject unfair, painful situations and insist on reasonable treatment. Sometimes expressing anger is necessary to clear the air and make yourself heard.

One day in mediation, Ellen, usually mild-mannered and undemanding, lost her temper when Tony kept insisting that he couldn't afford to pay $800 in child support, the amount the state would normally require of someone with his income. She pointed out with some wrath that, even with $800 and her own earnings, she and the children would be living on less income than he had just for himself. Tony, not used to Ellen's anger, was taken aback, but faced with the figures, he acknowledged that she had a point.

Anger can be a healthy reaction, or it can be abusive and destructive. When you express anger, don't personally attack your spouse. Ellen directed her anger at the suggestion that $800 was an unreasonable sum; she did not say that Tony was a cheapskate or an unloving father. Cursing and yelling also get you nowhere and are likely to sour the atmosphere and diminish your chances of reaching agreement.

Using Power Appropriately

Although using threats to intimidate your spouse is not useful in forging a fair settlement, you may at some point want to consider what power is available to you and use it.

Howard and Sharon were making little progress in mediating the issues of custody and child support because Howard insisted on having their two preschoolers half the time, and Sharon objected. She'd stayed home with the children all of their lives while Howard, very involved in his work, had shown little interest in them. He appeared ignorant of their routines and expressed scant concern about their welfare; his goal seemed to be to reduce his financial outlay for support.

In the past, Sharon had placated Howard and adjusted to his needs, but she refused to agree to a pattern that she believed would be damaging to the children. When Howard insisted on having them half the time, Sharon conferred with her lawyer to find out what a judge would do. Her attorney advised her that, because she'd been the primary caregiver and Howard had been an indifferent parent, a judge would almost certainly award her sole custody.

When she shared this information with Howard, he still refused to budge from his position. So Sharon told her lawyer to set the case for trial—a drastic step. She took the risk that she would have to endure an expensive custody battle if Howard continued to hold out.

However, Howard received the same analysis from his attorney, so he knew he would lose in court. Therefore, when Sharon made it clear that she would persist, he conceded. Two weeks before trial, they returned to mediation and settled their case.

Staying in the Present and Future

When making decisions about your divorce, focus on the present and future—not the past. Concentrating on finances and your children's needs will keep you on track in making realistic choices in mediation. Blaming for past failures will needlessly delay or possibly preclude agreements.

Staying focused can be hard work. When emotional issues arise, it may be difficult not to erupt with anger and a sense of injustice at the wrongs you've suffered at the hands of your spouse. You may be tempted to point out in scathing language how badly she's behaved and how unfairly you've been treated. However, doing so will probably make your spouse angry, defensive, and less likely than ever to agree to your proposals. Even if you succeed in gaining concessions brought on by her sense of guilt, she's likely to change her mind after leaving the session and talking to her lawyer.

You can raise emotionally charged issues if they're directly relevant to a point under discussion. For example, if your wife was repeatedly late picking up the children from day care, this fact may be pertinent when deciding who should have responsibility for that task in the future. If she spent a lot of community money on her boyfriend, that point may be relevant when deciding how to divide your property.

But her affair with another man, though very painful to you, may have nothing to do with who should have custody of the children or how retirement benefits should be divided. And berating her about her behavior, which the two of you have no doubt already discussed at great length elsewhere, will achieve no good ends in mediation.

If according to your lawyer your spouse's affair or gambling habits are directly relevant to your property division or custody issues, then raise those points in mediation. But do so in a way that raises the least amount of heat.

Talking About Your Needs, Not Your Spouse's Failings

Another way to avoid unnecessary rancor is to couch your comments in terms of your concrete needs rather than your spouse's bad behavior. For example: "As you can see from my list here, I need $1,000 a month to pay Timmy's expenses" is preferable to "Since you made me quit my job when we married and I now have no career, I can't support Timmy unless you pay me a lot of money."

Similarly, "I would like to pay you more child support, but I don't see how I can pay off our debts if I do" will probably work better than "If you hadn't run up our credit card bills the way you did, I could afford to pay more child support."

Pointing out your spouse's failures is likely to ignite a fight rather than lead to agreement. So stick to a clear statement of your own needs and avoid blaming your spouse in the process.

Caucusing

If your discussions are getting out of hand or you're afraid to raise sensitive subjects in the presence of your spouse, ask the mediator if you can "caucus." This means meeting separately with the mediator in another room. (She probably keeps one available for this purpose.) It's a technique frequently used in mediation when private communication is called for.

You may be afraid of your spouse's reaction to something you want to say or too mad to continue discussions together. If your anger makes it impossible to think straight, caucusing may give you an opportunity to calm down. It also gives you a chance to vent your anger in a way that won't damage the mediation. Your mediator can listen to your outrage and even sympathize with your feelings, and no harm is done.

You can also use caucusing to learn what the mediator thinks about your stance on a given issue. If the mediator is comfortable evaluating your case and is knowledgeable about family law, you may want to ask her privately how strong your position is for getting alimony or joint custody, or keeping all of your retirement.

Be sure to find out whether your comments in caucus will remain confidential. Can you say whatever you want without fear that the mediator will repeat it to your spouse? Or does your mediator believe that everything stated in caucus should be told to the other spouse? If she believes in full disclosure, keep that in mind when you caucus.

An Open Mind

I recently mediated a custody case in which the clients appeared with their attorneys. When Joe and Angie divorced two years ago, she let him keep custody of their ten-year-old son, Travis, because Joe lived with his older son (from a previous marriage), and Angie wanted the boys together. When the older boy went to live with his mother, Angie saw no reason why Travis should now live with Joe. Her lawyer asked that Angie have custody of her son.

Joe's lawyer argued against any change in Travis's living arrangements. The boy was doing very well in school, so why change things and disrupt his life?

Angie, however, had recently remarried and now lived with her two stepchildren close to Travis's age. She pointed out that Travis enjoyed these children and wanted to live with her.

Both sides had good reasons for their positions. Fortunately, no one had yet filed any legal documents in the case. An exchange of telephone calls between attorneys was all that had occurred. I say "fortunately" because neither side had yet become entrenched in a legal position and therefore reluctant to consider alternatives.

After our initial joint session, I met with Angie and her lawyer alone and learned that she was flexible about adjusting to new living arrangements. Rather than insisting that Travis live primarily with her, she was open to the possibility of his spending equal time with each parent.

I then met with Joe's lawyer, Gwen, to understand better her opposition to Angie's request. Gwen initially took the position that Angie had no legal grounds for seeking a change and that Joe therefore didn't need to consider her requests. She also pointed out all the ways in which Joe was the better parent and why Travis was better off with his father.

However, when we brought Joe into the room and asked him what he thought, he surprised us. "You know, Angie's a good mother. I'll give her that," Joe began. "And I suppose Travis really enjoys being over there. At my house, he's the only child, so he gets lots of attention, and I know he likes that. But at Angie's he's got other kids to play with, a family atmosphere, and I know he likes that too."

When I asked Joe what arrangements he'd be comfortable with, he suggested that Travis spend alternating weeks with each parent, though he was concerned about how Travis might handle the new schedule.

Gwen and I both were pleasantly surprised to hear Joe's suggestion. Gwen, believing that her client was opposed to change, had automatically taken the role of defending the status quo and fighting off any challenges. When she saw her mistake, however, she began working on a plan to please both parents. She suggested they try an alternating-week schedule for the next school semester as a trial to see how Travis adjusted. If he did well, they could make it a permanent arrangement. Angie readily agreed to this proposal.

In less than three hours of mediation the parties left with a written agreement detailing Travis's schedule and support for the next few months; the agreement provided for returning to mediation at the end of the semester to consider a permanent order.

This mediation went well because both parties were open minded; neither became locked in a position. Both were willing to consider alternatives, and both kept Travis's well-being paramount.

If the lawyers had remained adversarial, an agreement might not have been reached, but instead they listened to their clients and responded to their clients' willingness to cooperate.

Reasonable Goals

Sometimes clients enter mediation with unrealistic expectations. A husband may believe he's entitled to all of his retirement because he "earned it." A wife may believe she's entitled to support for the rest of her life because her husband "wronged" her by ending the marriage. Unless the other party agrees to these demands and gives up substantial legal rights, we won't make much headway in mediation.

Ed and Cathy were such a couple. Ed was a successful dentist, and Cathy was a part-time student. She wanted to attend law school but still needed two more years of undergraduate study.

Though Ed earned a good living, the two of them had developed a taste for luxuries that exceeded their income. They had bought an opulent home and run up considerable debt living in the style it suggested.

Both wanted to keep the house, but neither could afford it. Ed thought Cathy should take all their credit card debts considering that she'd incurred them by buying expensive clothes and fancy household items. Cathy thought Ed should not only pay off their credit cards but also make the house payments while she continued to live there and finish her education. Each of them blamed the other for the failure of their marriage and therefore felt entitled to whatever they wanted.

Both were so convinced of the correctness of their positions that I insisted they consult with attorneys before we met again. Their lawyers, I hoped, would educate them about their legal rights and return them to mediation with reasonable goals.

Indeed, they returned chastened and ready to talk realistically about their property and debts. We did eventually reach an agreement; they had to sell the house to pay their debts, and both had to adjust to more frugal lifestyles.

If you and your spouse don't agree on what's fair, one reasonable course is to consider how state law treats the issue and reach an agreement along those lines. After all, if you don't agree in mediation, you'll have to go to court, where the judge will apply state law to divide your estate. So why keep fighting for something you have no chance of getting in court? It's a waste of time and money.

Conferring with Your Attorney

As I discussed in Chapter Five, you'll be better prepared to mediate if you've first met with your attorney to discuss your legal rights. By being well informed you'll save time and mediator's fees.

It's also important to consult with your attorney as you proceed. If you run into rough spots and aren't sure whether to hold your ground or compromise, your lawyer can advise and support you.

Some clients rely on the gossip of relatives and neighbors to guide them in their own divorces. To do so is a mistake. Every divorce is different because the facts vary in every case. Your neighbor may be paying less child support because he makes less money, or has more time with his kids because he was more involved in their rearing.

Your lawyer is a far better source of advice. If reports from friends about their divorce raise questions in your mind about your own, talk to your lawyer.

Consulting Experts

In order to understand the tax and other financial implications of a possible settlement and to cope with the emotional upheaval of your family, make generous use of other professionals.

Financial Experts

A CPA may be a big help in explaining tax matters. Unless your attorney is also a tax expert, she may not be comfortable discussing the tax implications of your agreement, which can be significant. If one of you receives $10,000 in savings and the other a $10,000 IRA, that division is not equal: the IRA is subject to tax and the savings are not. And what about capital gains, dependency exemptions, and past tax liabilities?

You may want the assistance of a financial planner if you're dealing with large sums and know little about investments. She can help you determine how much income you'll need and what property will be most beneficial to you after divorce.

You may want to consult these experts before mediation, as issues arise, or after reaching a tentative agreement to be sure you haven't missed anything.

Therapist or Counselor

Divorce is very difficult for us all. For most, it's a time of great upheaval. You're changing your home, your parenting arrangements, your relationship with your spouse, and your financial condition; and you're doing all this while experiencing great pain, loss, and anxiety. It can be one of the most stressful times in your life.

Seeing a therapist while you go through these changes can be a great help. The therapist gives you a chance to sort out your feelings and vent your hurt and anger, providing a healthy outlet for your emotions outside of mediation, where they can be harmful.

The therapist may also help you understand what went wrong in your marriage so that you can avoid repeating mistakes. People going through divorce are usually convinced that they'll never be so foolish as to marry unwisely again, but most of us will repeat our errors if we don't carefully examine our behavior. That kind of examination is virtually impossible without the help of a trained therapist; it's like trying to remove your own gall bladder. Serious self-examination is not a simple matter.

A therapist can also help you guide your children through divorce. Children at this time are likely to experience complicated feelings not visible to their parents. A therapist may give you insight into those emotions and suggest ways to help your children survive and reduce the disruption of divorce.

If your spouse is willing, consider family therapy as well. The goal is not to save the marriage but to make the divorce as easy as possible on all of you. A family therapist helps each member of the family express feelings that may be hard to talk about elsewhere, and makes sure that each person is heard and respected. With the therapist's help, you and your spouse can explain your divorce to your children with love and reassurance. This experience may prevent misunderstandings that fester and cause pain.

Using Your Support System

The fear, anger, guilt, and confusion caused by divorce make this a particularly good time to stay close to sympathetic and supportive friends and family members. You'll need people who will spend time with you, listen to your concerns, and act as a sounding board.

If you don't have such people in your world, find them. Group therapy is an option. Reach out to people at work that you don't usually socialize with. Get to know your neighbors. Go to social affairs that you used to ignore. Check on support groups such as Parents Without Partners.

Your social contacts may have atrophied during your marriage. If so, this is the time to start rebuilding them.

10

What Doesn't Work

Caught up in the emotional drama of your divorce, you may be tempted to resort to old patterns and easy remedies. In this chapter I review inappropriate behavior I often see in mediation—power struggles, placating, threats, lying, and giving up—and the destructive results such behavior can cause.

Power Struggles

The most common and most destructive mistake divorcing couples make is to succumb to the lure of power struggles. Joey and Melinda offer a good example of what can happen. After two years of nasty litigation, they completed their divorce, but both still felt cheated and angry about the results. Two more trips to court to dispute their child support and property division left each convinced that the other was wildly unreasonable.

They came to me to mediate a change in child custody. Their teenage son, Ian, wanted to spend more time with his father, and both parents agreed that the change was appropriate. However, both also sought restitution for past injustices, and each was outraged by the other's demands.

In spite of strong feelings on both sides, we worked out a grudging agreement on almost everything. All that remained was Joey's demand for a few hundred dollars in back child support.

"Ian's been with me most of the last six months," Joey began, "yet I've been paying full child support. It's only fair that I get some of that back."

Melinda responded with arched eyebrows, "Aren't you forgetting that I paid for Ian's airplane ticket to meet you in Florida last year? You promised to pay me back but never did. And what about all those medical expenses you're supposed to reimburse me for?"

"You bought the airplane ticket because you made him miss the flight I'd paid for! And what medical expenses? I've never heard about medical expenses before!"

"Never heard of them?" Melinda was angrily searching through her box of papers. "Look! Here's a copy of the letter I sent you last month!" Triumphantly, she slapped the letter down on the table in front of him.

"I can't believe you're complaining about a few medical bills!" Joey retorted in disgust, waving the letter away. "Remember how much you stole from me in the divorce? Your lawyer cheated me out of $10,000 by lying about the house. And here you are whining about a few medical bills!"

Consider that these people had spent tens of thousands of dollars in lawyers' fees over the years and were paying my fee to help them sort out this controversy. Obviously, it would have made sense for both of them to forget this issue and put it to rest.

Yet neither would yield. Their deep resentments and years of fighting made them cling to this final issue as though all of their accumulated sufferings hung in the balance. To lose on this point was to admit defeat on everything.

Finally, Melinda, infuriated by Joey's demands, refused to return to mediation. Several months later, I ran into Joey at the courthouse; he said they were still battling in court.

When an issue takes on this disproportionate significance— when it comes to symbolize victory or defeat—you know you're caught in a power struggle.

When a couple argues tenaciously over who gets the child 51 percent of the time rather than 50 percent or 49 percent, the issue is not the child but winning. When they're fighting over fifty dollars of child support, they're concerned not with economic need but with victory.

If you find yourself in a power struggle, you'd best take a deep breath and step back. You may need a break from mediation, for a few minutes or a few days. When your anger has subsided, you'll be able to view the conflict more reasonably.

Remember your goals: achieving a reasonable settlement, promoting your children's welfare, and maintaining your dignity and mutual respect. Moral victory over your spouse is not a priority.

Remember too that insistence on one extra scrap of booty in your pile can lead to untold misery and expense for you and your family: months, if not years, of legal wrangling, family turmoil, and distressed children.

Even if you win and force your spouse to accept defeat, you may later regret it. A spouse who feels bested and humiliated isn't likely to be a friendly partner in coparenting your children. Consider as well your own integrity and peace of mind. Do you want to leave your marriage demeaned by your insistence on revenge?

Placating

Although I urge you to avoid power struggles and mindless insistence on victory, I don't suggest that you do whatever is necessary to satisfy your spouse. If he's making unreasonable demands and you're repeatedly agreeing to them to avoid a fight, you're probably making a mistake and laying the groundwork for later problems.

In Chapter Two, "Is Mediation the Best Choice for You?" I discuss impossible spouses—those who are bullies. If you're married to one, you may have constantly yielded to him to avoid confrontations. You may also have noticed that such placating does no good.

It may avoid an immediate fight, but it doesn't stop the bullying. As long as you keep giving in, he'll keep making demands.

If you continue to yield to unreasonable behavior, you'll probably end up with an agreement you regret, feeling cheated and humiliated. You may then be angry with your former spouse, your mediator, and your lawyer.

I recently mediated a divorce for Andy and Emma. Emma, a petite, blond, eager-to-please woman in her mid-thirties, followed Andy down the hall to my office. Lean and unsmiling, Andy seated himself and began laying out the terms of their divorce. Emma listened without comment. When pressed, she suggested timidly that she could use more child support, but Andy would have none of it. Emma looked at me appealingly but made no effort to argue her case.

When Andy remained resolute in response to my questions about their daughter's needs and his income, I insisted that Emma get legal advice. Her lawyer urged her to demand more financial benefits for herself and the children, but Emma ignored the advice; she was unwilling to stand up to Andy. The divorce proceeded, with Andy getting just what he wanted.

Two months later, I received a letter from Emma, berating me for having allowed her to agree to such terms. "You knew that $400 in child support was too low," she complained, "but you let me agree to it! How could you do that?"

You—not your lawyer or the mediator—are responsible for your agreement. If you want a fair settlement, you must take a stand on important issues and hold your ground. Your lawyer and mediator can help in this effort, but you must be prepared to confront your spouse's anger.

Of course, you must balance taking a firm stand with honestly evaluating your spouse's position. Many clients are convinced that their spouses are irrational when they don't appear so to me, perhaps because I'm considering the probable outcome in court whereas clients are considering their own idea of fairness.

So when you think your spouse is unreasonable, compare his demands with his legal rights and try to understand his idea of fairness. You may decide that either law or equity gives him a plausible argument.

If, on the other hand, your spouse is simply impossible, you may still decide you'd rather let him have what he wants than fight him. That's a legitimate decision and sometimes a wise one. Just be sure you've carefully considered what you'll be losing before you make that choice.

Sometimes walking away from a bully is the best course; sometimes standing up to him represents personal growth. It depends on what's at stake and what you're ready to handle. Some clients, for the first time ever, stand up to their spouses during divorce and are elated by their success and increased self-esteem. Others let their spouses get away with one-sided settlements to avoid unpleasantness, and I sometimes think that in their place I would do the same.

My point is that you should make your decision after careful consideration. If your acquiescence results from habit and fear rather than thoughtful deliberation, you are likely to regret it.

If your spouse is abusive, you may want to avoid mediation altogether. If he's violent and you don't feel safe negotiating with him, leave that job to your lawyer. You can't negotiate effectively when you're afraid of assault.

Threats

I often hear a client, in the heat of the moment, declare that if his spouse doesn't agree to his proposal he will humiliate her—usually by revealing embarrassing private matters in court. I've noticed that the ugly behavior thus exposed is rarely one-sided. If one spouse has had an affair, the other may have a drinking problem. If one has carelessly run up debts, the other may be unbearably controlling. Thus, threats of broadcasting embarrassing behavior in court will probably be met with reciprocal threats, and the venomous exchange will only diminish your chances of reaching an amicable settlement.

Lying

Some people are drawn to mediation because they think they can, in this setting, pull the wool over their spouses' eyes; others are simply tempted to be less than truthful when asked hard questions.

Spouses, who know each other so well, seem to sense when the other is lying, and they immediately lose trust. Settlement depends on that trust; when trust is damaged, mediation may end, leaving you to face the expense and trauma of litigation. But now your spouse, convinced of your duplicity, will take every legal step possible to avoid being cheated—which means more lawyer time, more of your time, and more stress on everyone.

Larry thought that the informal tone of mediation would allow him to hide assets. But his wife, Claire, knew from his secretiveness and their lifestyle that they owned more than he was revealing. Because of her suspicions, I suggested that each file in court a sworn inventory, listing all their assets and debts. Larry refused.

Claire, understandably incensed, went to her lawyer, who formally demanded all of Larry's business and bank records. Larry continued to try to dodge disclosure, so hearings followed. Claire's lawyer convinced the judge that because Larry had refused to cooperate, he should pay the $20,000 in legal fees needed to define and value their estate.

Claire's lawyer was then able to conduct extensive discovery and establish high values for assets that Larry had not acknowledged or had undervalued. At trial, the judge, still unhappy with Larry's behavior, awarded Claire a hefty share of the community assets.

Karen was another client who tried to hide important information. Something about her reluctance to talk about her new boyfriend and an unexplained medical bill made her husband, Jack, suspicious. Under pressure, Karen finally admitted that she was pregnant with her boyfriend's child. Furious, Jack refused to continue mediation; the parties retained attorneys and divorced the hard way.

Had Karen revealed the truth early on and faced her husband's anger, mediation might have succeeded. Her attempts to deceive made it harder for Jack to accept the situation and made mediation impossible.

Lying doesn't pay. Even if you're one of the few to get away with it, living with lies will only erode your self-respect.

Giving Up Too Soon

Some clients, in anger and frustration, leave mediation because they believe their spouses are so unreasonable that they will never reach an agreement. Or, piqued by their spouses' demands, they encourage their lawyers to escalate hostilities, thus destroying the atmosphere of trust and cooperation required for mediation.

Before you decide that mediation isn't working, *ask the mediator if he agrees*. He's in the best position to evaluate your progress. Having seen dozens of couples in a situation much like yours, he may think that you're proceeding normally and will soon have everything worked out.

If your mediator recommends you both confer with attorneys before returning to mediation, he's not suggesting that they take over the case; he thinks legal advice will help you mediate more effectively.

Remember too that according to national statistics 85 percent of all cases submitted to mediation settle there. And if you start mediation before you become embroiled in litigation, your chances are even better.

Part III

Protecting Your Children

11

Your Children's Needs

Having gone through divorce myself, I vividly remember my own anger and how hard it was to shield my four-year-old daughter from those feelings. I was not always successful. Because of my experience, I sympathize greatly with the struggle of other divorcing parents to protect their children from adult conflicts. When we're absorbed in our own painful dramas, it's often hard to keep our children's best interests in mind.

Yet we must, for although we may recover from our divorces in a few months or a few years, our children may never fully recover if we handle the divorce badly.

In mediation, you'll be making decisions about custody and child support; but before we look at those legal issues in detail in the next chapter, let's consider some of the underlying questions with which you'll be grappling:

- How important are both parents to your children?

- What are the pressures that cause you to lose sight of what's best for your children?

- What do they need from you now?

- Where can you get helpful guidance?

Do They Really Need Both Parents?

Most of us have great hopes for our children. We want them to become healthy, independent adults; we want them to be able to form lasting and loving relationships; and we hope that they'll someday express their interests and talents in a productive, satisfying vocation.

Can your children achieve these goals without your spouse's help? Perhaps, but if that other parent is not involved in their lives, their road to adulthood will be rockier, their chances of achieving healthy emotional maturity reduced.

Sometimes it's difficult for us to see how someone who has failed to meet *our* emotional needs may nevertheless meet crucial needs of our children. However, that parent is their mother or father forever, and only she or he can provide fundamental elements of parenting that our children require. Even if that parenting is done imperfectly, it may be crucial to our children.

Rosemary, a friend, told me how important her father was to her after her parents' divorce. In spite of his many failings—he was a poor money manager, a womanizer, and generally irresponsible—he loved his daughter. Rosemary adored her father and lived for the days he spent with her.

"Mother remarried, and I had a good stepfather," she remarked, "but Dad was special. He encouraged me to stick with my science classes and eventually to become a veterinarian. I don't think I'd have tried if he hadn't kept telling me I could do it."

Her mother was justifiably angry with the man for making her married life miserable and frequently said so. Reflecting on her mother's anger, Rosemary said, "I can understand why Mother didn't like him; he was a lousy husband. But her anger at him just made me feel guilty and ashamed for loving him."

The Children's Need to Respect Both Parents

Rosemary's remarks raise another significant point: your children need not only *time* with each parent but *respect* for each as well. In venting our anger, we may say hurtful things that our children don't need to hear. In fact, hearing such comments is painful and confusing for them.

Rosemary knew that her father had serious faults, but the contempt and disdain she heard from her mother caused her to think less not only of him but of herself as well. After all, she loved this father who was apparently so despicable, and she was his child. If he was so flawed, she must be too.

Jeremy, a young man whose parents had divorced when he was eight, told me of another way parents' acrimony and lack of mutual respect can damage their children. "My folks had a huge custody fight. Dad won, and he was so mad at Mom by the time it was over that he wouldn't speak to her. He told me some really awful things about her—other men, drugs, lying, and so on—and even said she didn't really love me."

His father's anger and the stories about his mother so upset Jeremy that he refused to visit her. "I knew Dad didn't want me to go with her, and I thought I could show that I was a man like him by treating my mother like a criminal. So I barely saw her for several years."

As a teenager, Jeremy began having serious problems; he got into fights and was caught stealing from neighbors. His father then turned to his mother for help, hoping that she might provide some relief from his constant battles with his son.

"I fought with her, too," Jeremy continued, "but she hung in there and made me straighten up. She didn't give up on me. I realized she really did love me, and she was strong. We had a rough time there for a while, but we made it. I'm graduating from college next spring, and I can promise you it wouldn't have happened without her."

When children know that their parents are angry with each other, they may believe that their loyalty to one requires them to reject the other and to turn their backs on the love and nurturing that parent can offer.

Acknowledging the Importance
of Your Children's New Homes

When I divorced over twenty years ago, I gave little thought to my daughter's continuing relationship with her father. I moved to another city, began a new career, and left it to him to figure out how he was going to see his child. I didn't much care whether he did so frequently or not.

I also didn't give much thought to what kind of accommodations she had when she stayed with her father. Her home was with me, and her brief "visits" with him seemed to me unimportant.

I now realize my mistake. I know that those trips to her father's house were a major force in her development. She needed to feel that she was a valued part of his life, and she couldn't do that if he didn't demonstrate her importance by seeing her regularly, paying attention to her, and arranging his home and lifestyle to reflect her significance. She felt slighted, for example, when he didn't dedicate his spare bedroom to her but kept it as a guest room; she indeed felt like a "guest."

He and I both failed to regard his house and his parenting as equal in importance to mine. I also did little to encourage her father to attend her school activities and stay informed about and involved in her new life. If he saw little of her, that would be acceptable to me.

Because of these assumptions we made, our daughter felt insecure in her relationship with her father and spent years trying to prove that she was worthy of his affection and esteem. I, of course, blamed him for not paying more attention to her, but I also failed in not making his access to her easier and not acknowledging the importance of his fathering.

Looking back at the pain we caused our daughter, I know I would do things differently if given a second chance. I would sit down with her father and discuss what we both could do to allow her more time with him and to make her feel that his home was truly hers. I would have urged him to attend her school activities and kept him informed of her achievements and interests.

Although it's difficult to see past the heat and confusion of divorce, I urge you to set aside your strong emotions about your spouse when making important decisions about your children's future. The story of Maria and Virgil illustrates how one couple struggled with the issue of two homes for their children.

"Why do you need any of the children's furniture?" Maria asked Virgil. "The girls will be living with me. They won't need much at your house."

Virgil gritted his teeth. "They won't be camping out, you know. They'll need beds and stuff, just like at your place."

"Well, your brother has those twin beds in his attic. You could use those."

"The ones I slept in as a kid? Those beds are falling apart!" Virgil exploded.

Because this issue hinged on Maria's respect for the children's home with their father, I decided to caucus and asked Virgil to wait in another room while I talked to Maria. I wanted to explore her feelings about the girls' staying with their father, and I thought she would be more candid in Virgil's absence.

"How do you feel about the girls staying with their dad?" I asked after Virgil left.

"Oh, he won't pay much attention to them. He's making a big deal of it now, but it's all show. He'll lose interest in them."

"Do you want him to be involved with them?" I asked.

Maria looked uncomfortable. "Well, sure. I'm just being realistic. I know the man. But you know, I don't care if he does fade out of our lives. We can get along without him."

"Maria, did you see much of your dad when you were growing up?"

Her eyes met mine immediately, and I knew I'd hit a nerve. Then she looked down.

"No. My parents divorced when I was five. My father didn't come around much, but we got along OK, I guess. It was hard, but we managed."

"Would you have liked to have seen him more?"

"Oh, yes. I missed him something awful. I'd call and ask him to come get me, but he usually didn't show up. I thought about him a lot."

We sat silently for a moment, while Maria remembered her father and her eyes grew moist.

"Maria, what kind of relationship would you like for your girls to have with their father?"

"Well, of course I want them to have a good relationship with Virgil. I just don't think he'll follow through."

"You may be right," I acknowledged. "You know him better than I do. What do you think we could do to encourage him to spend more time with them—so they won't miss him the way you missed your dad?"

"Well, I don't know if the girls really want to spend time with him. I mean, their friends are all at my house. They don't know anyone over there."

"Could something be done to make his house feel more like home—so they'd be comfortable there?"

"I see where you're going." She gave me a wry smile. "You figure if he has some of their furniture, they'll like being there more. And then maybe they'll have a better relationship."

"What do you think?"

"Oh, maybe you're right. I guess it wouldn't hurt to try."

When Virgil joined us again, we continued to talk about not only the furniture but other ways that the girls might make a place for themselves at their father's—getting to know neighborhood children, exploring stores in the area, helping their dad decorate his house.

Maria was not comfortable with all of this. It was clearly hard for her to let go of her role as the girls' "real" parent, but she wrestled with her discomfort and did what she thought was best for her children.

How the Children's Needs Get Lost

Sometimes, overwhelmed by our own needs, we lose sight of those of our children. We may even convince ourselves that we're acting on their behalf when we're really taking care of ourselves. In this section, I'll look at some of the ways that can happen.

Children as a Vehicle for Parental Anger and Control

Most people going through a divorce feel some anger and resentment and, if they will admit it, would like to punish their spouses for the pain they've caused. That's human nature. We may be ashamed of such feelings, but most of us experience them nonetheless.

That desire to punish often gets acted out with the children serving as the paddle. I've seen fathers seek joint custody to get even with wives who have hurt them. And I've seen wives attempt to limit their husbands' access to the children as revenge for the pain and humiliation of divorce.

Parents engaged in such power struggles are rarely aware of their true motivation. They insist that their demands and denials are "for the good of the children" when they're actually bent on winning one last argument in the continuing marital quarrel.

Of course, sometimes parents *do* need to take firm stands on how much time the children spend with each, but a few more days a month with one parent or the other are not likely to have a serious impact. What matters most to the children is that they see enough of both parents to benefit from their love, guidance, and attention; they also need to know that their parents treat each other with respect and consideration.

A Spouse's New "Significant Other"

Often a parent is distressed when the children are exposed to the other parent's new romantic interest, insisting that this intrusion is harmful to the children.

Although a premature introduction of new partners into the children's lives may indeed be disturbing to the children (particularly if the parents have recently separated), the other parent may be more uncomfortable with the new arrangements than the children are.

For most people, divorce means forming new relationships. Although the children should meet these new friends gradually and after an opportunity to adjust to their parents' separation, both children and parents will need eventually to adapt to new lifestyles and friendships. Therefore, in mediation your discussions of these new friends should focus on *how*, rather than *whether*, they should be introduced to the children.

Keep in mind too that if one parent is bothered by the other parent's new friend, he is likely to convey his distress to the children, thereby upsetting them as well. Therefore, use tact and discretion in bringing new "significant others" into your children's and their other parent's lives. And remember to use the same tact and discretion when discussing the subject in mediation.

The Need for Stability in the Children's Lives

Sometimes one parent resists the other's request for more time with the children in the belief that the children need stability more than additional time with the other parent, that too much bouncing back and forth will be confusing to them.

Experts disagree on the importance of stability versus large amounts of time with both parents, but they do agree that the need for stability is greater for young children and diminishes as the children grow. They also agree on the following:

- Children need sufficient time with each parent to maintain a healthy relationship with both.

- Children need not spend half their time with each parent, although such a division is sometimes desirable.

- Children's well-being is affected more by the parents' attitudes about sharing custody than by how much time they spend with each parent (assuming that the children have a base amount of time with each parent).

For example, let's assume that after we subtract the child's sleeping hours and time in school or day care, sixty hours a week remain. Let's further assume that each parent should spend at least one-quarter of that time, or fifteen hours, with the child. That leaves thirty hours a week to be apportioned between the parents. Most parents, to their credit, can divide this time without a great deal of strain, but others end up at loggerheads over the issue.

The experts suggest that how much of that remaining time the children spend with each parent is not so important as how comfortable the parents are with the division. If children sense that their parents feel at ease with the schedule, the children will adapt to it. If they sense that their parents are resentful or concerned, the children will feel the arrangement is unsafe.

The Overly Involved Parent

I recently mediated a divorce between Ken and Lillian, two intelligent and likeable parents, both very fond of their nine-year-old daughter, Jessie. However, as Ken talked enthusiastically about his time with Jessie after the divorce, Lillian became increasingly agitated. She and Jessie, it appeared, were very close, and she was afraid of their relationship being undermined by Ken.

"I've always made all the decisions about Jessie," she pointed out to her husband. "When you taught her to ride a bike, I had to pick out the right bicycle; the one you chose was too dangerous. If I hadn't been there, she might have been hurt. I don't see how I can agree for her to be away from me more than a few hours at a time. It's just not safe."

"I know your relationship with Jessie is very important to you," Ken acknowledged, "but it's only reasonable that she be with me every other weekend. The court would give me that at least."

Lillian was greatly distressed. "How can you do this to me?" she demanded. "You know it would kill me to lose Jessie that way!"

Clearly Lillian felt she needed an exclusive relationship with her child for her own good, not Jessie's. Her role as mother had become so important to her that she couldn't conceive of life without that close connection. Jessie's interests, however, had been lost.

To my disappointment, Ken yielded, hoping that Lillian would relax in time and allow him to spend more time with Jessie. I hope she did.

Again, mediation discussions must focus on the *child's* best interests, not the parents'. A child as enmeshed as Jessie was with one parent is in danger of being emotionally smothered and is particularly in need of a strong relationship with the other parent, who can guide her toward independence.

Family and Social Influences

I once mediated a divorce in which the parents of two elementary school children were fighting over custody. The case had been bitterly disputed and was set for trial three days later.

As we explored the possibility of joint custody and sharing equal time, both parents insisted on having more time with the children than the other. Though neither claimed the other was an inadequate parent, both dug in their heels in their determination to have the children at least one more hour per month than the other.

"Why?" I asked the mother in a private session. "Help me understand why it is important to you *not* to have equal time sharing?"

Her response was, "What will the neighbors think?"

This mother's bluntness and candor surprised me. Most people would not so baldly acknowledge their fear of the social disapproval attendant upon "losing" custody, but that fear is nevertheless a powerful if unspoken influence on many a divorcing parent.

The mother in this case continued to fight for sole custody at trial and lost. The father was named the primary parent, reducing the mother's time with her children to considerably less than she could have received in mediation. Her fear of social disapproval caused her even greater embarrassment, several thousand dollars more in attorneys' fees, and deeper scars in her relationship with the child's father.

The father was, of course, equally adamant about not yielding, though his opposition seemed to be based more on the desire to maintain supremacy over his wife than on fear of social disapproval.

I recall another case in which the grandmothers were the driving forces toward litigation. Paul and Cicily were both young, and they depended on their parents to pay their attorneys' fees. Although both of them loved their two-year-old son, were good parents, and needed each other to coordinate his care, each grandmother was intent on her child having sole custody.

Unfortunately, Paul and Cicily lacked the maturity and independence to withstand these pressures. When the case was eventually tried, each side had spent about $25,000. Cicily won custody, but she lost a cooperative coparent to help her raise her son.

Often unstated but nevertheless powerful, these influences from family and friends may require a great deal of strength to resist.

The Disinterested Spouse

Occasionally I see one parent, usually the mother, trying to persuade her spouse to spend *more* time with the children. The father in these cases shows little interest in his children, in spite of his wife's urgings. This too is a power struggle. When the husband realizes that his wife wants him to spend more time with the children, he asserts himself by withdrawing. The harder she pushes, the more he resists.

If you're the wife in this scenario, it won't help to keep pushing. If the father isn't eager to participate in his children's rearing, you can't make him. You can provide him with information about their activities and be cooperative when he wants to see them, but insisting on his involvement will only intensify a power struggle that he can win only by withdrawing.

If you are the father in this situation, understand that your attention to and love for your children are crucial to their healthy development.

Role Modeling for Your Children

Children need parents who present models of healthy adult behavior. As they observe your divorce, they'll learn how adults resolve conflicts. If you successfully mediate your divorce, your children will learn that people can seriously disagree and still maintain their mutual respect and affection.

Children also observe how their parents handle separation. Will they witness a violent and vitriolic division, or will they see two adults accomplish the transition with grace and compassion? The choice you make may influence how your children approach the major separations in their own lives.

Getting the Advice of Experts

When I divorced, my daughter said little about the divorce, so I gratefully concluded that she was not seriously concerned. I thought it best if I also said little, not wanting to create problems where none existed.

I was wrong. Years later, when I remarried and the three of us sought counseling to work out our new family relationships, I learned that my daughter had seriously misunderstood the reasons for the divorce. She had blamed herself and suffered more than I knew from the loss.

I wish I had received expert advice at the time of divorce so that I could have helped her understand that she was blameless and very much loved by her father and me. My failure to do so caused her years of unhappiness.

Because children sometimes find it difficult to articulate their feelings and may be afraid to speak openly of their insecurities, I urge you to get expert guidance. You might talk to a counselor about how you and your spouse can make the divorce easier on your children, or you can ask a therapist to meet with the children so she can help you understand their needs. Expert guidance is most beneficial if both parents work closely with a mental health professional, but if your spouse won't participate, you and your children will still benefit from the therapist's advice.

Books can also be sources of help. When I divorced, it didn't occur to me that I might find help for my daughter at the library. Though I knew I was not handling things well, I thought I just had to muddle through as best I could. I was wrong again. Many people highly experienced in helping children through divorce have written books to help the rest of us.

In the For Further Reading section near the end of this book, I review some literature that might help you and help your children as they accept your divorce and adjust to their new family situation. Some of the books are for parents and some are meant to be read to your children or given to them to read, depending on their ages.

I strongly urge you to sample these books. They can make a world of difference in helping you and your children successfully navigate the turbulent waters of divorce.

12

Planning Your Children's Future Care

Once, when I asked a couple in mediation about their children's future care, the husband looked me in the eye and soberly replied, "Actually, we were hoping you'd take them."

Although this couple was relaxed enough to joke, most parents find these deliberations difficult. Their desire to protect and provide for their children conflicts with fear of fading from their children's lives or endangering their own financial security.

I attempt in this chapter to allay such concerns by exploring a variety of healthy parenting arrangements that allow you both to remain involved with your children and fairly share their expenses. As we consider different styles of coparenting, we'll look at the time you each spend with your children, how you share their expenses, and how you will make decisions about their care.

Remember: although you and your spouse are divorcing each other, neither of you is divorcing your children. You'll both continue to parent, just in a different context. You'll now have two households—each with a separate home, budget, and style of decision making.

In mediation, you work out a plan for those two households to cooperatively provide physical, emotional, spiritual, and financial care for your children.

How Much Time Should
Your Children Spend with Each Parent?

Experts believe that children under age three need a stable primary home with one parent and frequent—if possible, daily—contact with the other. Because young children have short memory spans, frequent contacts are essential.

As children grow, they can tolerate longer stays with each parent. The question is how to allocate your children's time as they mature.

Allocating Your Children's Time with Each Parent

How do you decide on a schedule for the children? When are they to be at each home? Some fortunate couples don't need a schedule; they trade the kids back and forth depending on their own needs or the children's wishes. But most couples need a plan, and most children want to know what their week will look like.

Indeed, whether you feel the need for one or not, the court in your state may require a detailed schedule in your paperwork so that if the two of you don't agree later, your rights are spelled out in your orders.

Here are some thoughts that can help as you work out such a plan.

1.   *Who's been their primary caretaker?* The first consideration in planning your children's future is their past. Who gets them up in the morning and off to school or day care? Who picks them up in the afternoon and makes sure their homework is done? Who takes them to the doctor and stays home with them when they're sick? Who gets them to bed in the evening? Who prepares their meals and sees to it that they eat properly? When both parents are in the room, which one does the child look to for comforting and care? In short, to whom is the child "bonded"?

Although some couples share child care equally, most don't. Typically, one parent assumes primary responsibility and the other helps. Sometimes, however, couples disagree about how much each has been involved in parenting.

Chris and Alicia were such a couple. When I asked how they'd cared for their three girls, Chris immediately responded.

"Oh, it's been pretty even. You know, we both do stuff with them. Alicia gets them up and dressed, and I drop them off at school. We share the work."

Alicia looked surprised. "Chris! I do most of that! I don't just get them up and dressed. I pick them up from school, I cook their meals, I help them with their homework, I put them to bed. You don't usually get home from work before eight!"

Under pressure, Chris acknowledged that Alicia did all these things, but pointed out that he played with the girls on Sunday afternoons.

This sort of exchange is not uncommon in mediation. For a number of reasons (which we'll examine later in this chapter), parents may exaggerate their participation in child rearing.

Because your children are likely to feel the loss of their primary caretaker most keenly, it's important to be honest in determining which of you has provided most of their care. You'll not want to suddenly disrupt their relationship with that parent.

Staying with their primary parent is most important for younger children, but an abrupt shift in living arrangements can be confusing and frightening to a child of any age. Because divorce is unsettling to a child under the best of circumstances, it's unwise to aggravate the situation by changing primary caretakers as well.

Nevertheless, changing parental roles may be called for if

• The child is old enough to handle the shift

• Both parents agree that it's better for the child

- The parent to assume the larger role has the time, preparation, and inclination for it

- The change is gradual

Of course, if parents equally shared child care before divorce, then doing so afterwards should not be a problem. Indeed, a marked change would be likely to distress the child.

2.   *Should child support be a factor?* As Chris and Alicia turned to the subject of their daughters' support, Chris became agitated.

"I don't see why we need child support. I'll have the girls half the time, so I'll be paying for their expenses as much as Alicia will."

"I haven't said I've agreed to your having them half the time," Alicia retorted. "I'm not sure that's a good idea. You've never taken care of them before. And I know I can't make it without support."

Unfortunately, parents sometimes seek more time with their children (or resist requests for more time) out of concern about child support. I'll discuss later in this chapter factors that affect child support, but how much time each parent has the children is only one of those factors. And parents should *never* request or deny access to a child in order to manipulate the amount of child support.

A parent arguing for custody isn't likely to say that money is the real issue, so if you believe your spouse is acting based on financial considerations rather than concern for your children, say so. Make your point as tactfully as possible and then insist on focusing on what's best for your children—without regard to child support.

3.   *Parents' and children's daily schedules.* You can resolve many disputes by realistically examining everyone's schedules.

To illustrate, I recently mediated a case in which the parents couldn't agree on who should have primary custody. When we examined their schedules, I learned that the mother worked during the day and planned to hire an expensive nanny to baby-sit. The father, on the other hand, had a flexible work schedule; he could care for the child on weekdays, while working evenings and weekends. By fixating on custody, these parents had overlooked the obvious solution of sharing child care according to their schedules and saving the cost of the nanny.

Write down your children's daily routines and compare them with each parent's. When do the kids need to arrive at day care or school? When do they need to be picked up at the end of the day? As the children grow, they'll probably become involved in extracurricular activities—sports, piano, school clubs, scouts, and so forth. Which parent's schedule better accommodates each task?

When you must adjust parental schedules to meet your children's needs, try to do so in a way that allows both of you to stay involved in their activities.

4. *Need for relief.* Keep in mind too that both parents need help in child rearing; it's a hard job for either to tackle single-handedly. If one parent wants more time with the children, the other has more opportunity for rest and recreation. To be an effective parent, you need time for yourself; if you're working full-time and providing most or all of your children's care, you'll probably be exhausted.

Your children will feel the effects of your fatigue. They'll have one wilted, semiattentive parent instead of two rested and responsive parents.

5. *The children's wishes.* For children, divorce is a catastrophe visited on them by adults. Though their lives are changed dramatically and permanently, they have no control over any of it. Allowing children to say and perhaps decide where they want to live acknowledges their power, their dignity, and their importance.

You don't have to do whatever your children want—as the adults, you and your spouse are responsible for making the decisions. But you can alleviate your children's feelings of powerlessness by asking them what they want, listening carefully, and giving their wishes high priority.

On the other hand, if the two of you are in a custody dispute, asking your children where they want to live places them in a precarious position. To choose between warring parents is dangerous; they could antagonize and alienate a parent whose love they need. And if they feel responsible for a contested custody decision, guilt will add an additional burden to their shoulders.

If children feel pressured into saying they prefer to live with one parent, they probably won't speak honestly; they'll say what they think that parent wants to hear. They may do this even when both parents are genuinely trying to do what's best for their children.

A professional counselor, trained to gently explore children's feelings, may be helpful in this situation. Clients are, however, sometimes wary of this suggestion. Alicia was one such client.

"The girls may *say* they want to live with Chris because he's being so sweet to them right now," she explained, "but he's not usually like this. He's just trying to avoid child support. He tells them how lonely he is, so they feel sorry for him and think they ought to stay with him."

Alicia may have been right about the girls. If so, a good therapist will find out. A professional counselor will use psychological testing, play therapy, and other techniques to look past the children's words to the emotions behind them. To understand the family dynamics, the therapist will also interview both parents and observe their interactions with their children.

Be Specific

In the old days, a divorce decree stated that the noncustodial parent would have the children "at all reasonable times agreed upon by the parties." That was it.

Today that portion of the final order may require ten or twelve pages, detailing exactly when each parent may have the children. Such detail is necessary in case parents later disagree about schedules; if their order doesn't specify the times for each, they could end up fighting in court. Parents can still, by agreement, modify their schedules for having the children, but their court order describes their legal rights in the event they don't agree on something else.

"Standard" Schedules

Some states have set up "standard visitation schedules" for the parent who doesn't have primary custody. If your state has such standards and you don't agree on another schedule, the judge will probably order these statutory guidelines. They usually consist of alternate weekends, one evening during the week, and half the children's holidays and summer vacations.

In mediation you're free to use standard schedules or discard them in favor of something that works better for your family.

Weekly Patterns

The pattern of the children staying with one parent during the school week and the other on certain weekends has some strong advantages. It allows children to have a stable home life, particularly during their school week, and gives both parents weekend time with their children.

Occasionally a couple considers giving one parent *all* the weekend time. That's probably not a good idea, because both parents occasionally want to be with their children on a weekend—for a short vacation, a visit with out-of-town guests, a trip to see relatives, or just a chance to enjoy their children at leisure.

Some couples want to divide their children's time evenly in each home in a variety of ways: by alternating weeks, half-weeks, months, semesters, or even years. Keep in mind that the more complicated the schedule for changing homes, the more disruptive and confusing it may be to your children, particularly if they repeatedly change during the school week.

One way for each parent to have roughly equal visitation time is for the children to live with one during the school year and with the other during the summer. The parent who has primary care of the children during the summer also has them for extra-long weekends during the school year (Thursday night to Monday morning); the other parent has them for regular weekends during the summer (Friday night to Sunday night). If holidays are divided equally, the children will spend about half their time with each parent and still have a stable home environment.

Summer and Holidays

Should you split your children's summers equally between two homes? Or should their regular weekly schedule continue, with each parent having two or three weeks of vacation with the children? Or, if one parent spends less time with the children during the school year, should that parent have them more in the summer? You and you spouse can arrange your children's summer schedules in whatever way works for you all.

Your children may also divide their holiday time equally between their two homes. For example, they can spend Thanksgiving with one of you this year and with the other the next. They can be with each of you for one week of winter vacation, arranged so that they alternate Christmas Day in each home. Or, if your traditions differ, they may spend Christmas Eve with one of you every year and Christmas Day with the other. Some couples prefer to split Thanksgiving and Christmas Days so that their children spend time with each parent on those days. Others give each parent the entire two-week winter holiday in alternating years.

Is it important that each of you spend time with your children on other holidays, their birthdays, or other regular family gatherings? If so, be sure to discuss these dates with your spouse and mediator so that your final orders cover them.

And remember—these detailed schedules are your fall-back position. The two of you can always ignore them and work things out according to your needs. Only if you don't agree to something else do these schedules become legally binding.

Supervised Care of Your Children

If your spouse has had an abusive relationship with your children, you may want to require that his time with them be supervised, probably by a family member, a neutral person, or an agency. In many cities organizations exist for exactly that purpose—to supervise a parent's visit and to provide a safe place for parents to exchange their children.

In my city, Kids Exchange, Inc., provides such a service. A nonprofit organization housed in a centrally located, comfortable older home, it gives children a pleasant place to play with their parents or to wait for a parent to pick them up. Staff members supervise parents when required by court order. Your mediator will know about such a place in your city.

Because supervised visitation is likely to be a highly offensive topic to your spouse, approach the subject cautiously. But if you believe your children require a neutral, safe environment in which to visit their other parent, talk to your mediator about it.

How Much Child Support Is Reasonable?

Most divorcing parents are seriously concerned about child support. Will one of them have to pay it? How much will it be?

Guidelines for Child Support

In most states, courts apply a mathematical formula to one or both parents' incomes to determine fair child support. The formula, known as "guidelines," varies from state to state, so ask your mediator or a family law attorney about what guidelines, if any, apply to you and your spouse.

In developing these guidelines, legislators assume that children will live primarily with one parent, who pays most of their expenses—clothing, meals, school supplies, haircuts, day care, extracurricular activities, gifts for other children, and so on. That parent will probably also maintain a larger residence and pay more for utilities, car maintenance, and gasoline. One purpose of child support is to reimburse the parent who incurs these expenses.

Another purpose is to equalize the living standards in the two homes so that children aren't deprived if they live primarily with the lower-earning parent. Although guidelines *attempt* to even living standards, they don't necessarily equalize the lifestyles of the two families. Men typically enjoy a higher standard of living after divorce than do women, even after paying child support, because men typically receive higher salaries. But guidelines try to ensure that the children share the benefits of either parent's higher earnings.

I recently saw *A Simple Twist of Fate*, a movie based on George Eliot's *Silas Marner*. In this contemporary remake, the natural father of a girl he abandoned in infancy tries to win legal custody of her from the man who raised her. The judge wrestles with whether to give custody to the poor man who has lovingly raised her or to her wealthy natural father, who provided none of her care.

In real life the judge would have no dilemma. The child would continue to live with her adopted father, and her natural father would pay support. Thus she would have the advantages of both worlds—the love and nurturance of one and the financial resources of the other. Of course, the natural father would probably be given an opportunity to spend time with his child and to support her emotionally as well.

I don't mean to paint an idealistic picture. Very often one parent's income, even when augmented by child support, is inadequate to create a home similar to the other parent's. My point is simply that child support is intended to spread income between the two households so that the child does not suffer from a marked disparity.

The Effect of Equal Time Sharing

Because child-support guidelines presume that children dwell primarily with one parent, they may not be appropriate when children spend equal or nearly equal time with both.

If both parents provide comparable housing and pay about the same amount for household expenses, child support should be lower than usual or not awarded at all. How much lower? When should it disappear altogether? There are no fixed answers. I can only point out issues to consider when determining child support in these situations.

1. *How much time children spend with each parent.* You may remember Chris's earlier objection to paying support: "If the children are with each of us half the time, why should we have child support?" He has a point. If he's absorbing half the cost of the children's groceries and other household expenses, his obligation to pay support should diminish. But how much time each parent has the children is not the only consideration.

2. *Who pays which expenses.* Even when parents have their children for equal periods of time, one may be paying certain expenses that the other doesn't—clothes, haircuts, extracurricular activities, and insurance. If so, money may need to change hands to compensate the paying parent.

Some couples avoid this imbalance by equitably assigning expenses to each parent—for example, one buys clothes and haircuts and another pays for medical insurance and extracurricular activities.

Other parents buy whatever they think necessary for the children and then even up their accounts every month. How much one parent reimburses the other can be subject to a cap. For example, if Dad is worried that Mom may spend too much on the kids' clothing, they can agree that he doesn't have to reimburse her for more than his share of $1,000 per year (or whatever amount they think reasonable) for clothing expenses.

Still others decide before divorce how much the children's monthly expenses will probably be and agree on a child support amount to cover the paying parent's share. For example, Margo and Phil estimated that she would spend, on the average, about $1500 more every month for their children's monthly expenses than would Phil, so they agreed that Phil would pay Margo half that amount in monthly child support.

Which option you choose depends on several factors: how much you trust your spouse to incur reasonable expenses, whether you think it practical to keep receipts and make monthly accountings, and whether you can agree on a reasonable monthly payment.

Because state law may make some options less enforceable than others, consult your attorney before making final decisions. (Later in this chapter, I discuss enforceability in more detail.)

3.   *Relative parental incomes.* Each parent's share of the children's expenses might be 50 percent, or it might be based on the parents' earnings. If the mother is a dentist and makes $150,000 a year, and the father makes $30,000 a year as a school teacher, it makes sense for the mother to pay more than half of their children's expenses. If her share is based on her relative earnings, the mother will pay 83 percent.

Some object to a strictly proportional distribution of expenses when one parent's income is very high, say over $100,000 a year. How much of that parent's income does the other truly need to pay their children's reasonable expenses? There is no hard and fast answer, though your state law may provide guidance. In mediation you're free to distribute your incomes in any way you agree is fair—so long as your children aren't deprived. However, a judge must find that the amount upon which you have agreed is in your children's best interest. If you decide that one of you will pay little or none of your children's expenses, be prepared to explain to the judge how your children benefit from that decision—a very difficult, if not impossible, task.

Remember, the agreement you reach in mediation will be drafted into a legal document that a judge must ultimately sign. In my area, the judge will approve almost anything a couple agrees to—with the exception of child support; she will always check to make sure that the child support is reasonable. And it's hard to convince her that it's in your children's best interest to receive little or no support from one parent.

Aside from the likelihood that a judge won't approve such an arrangement, it's probably unwise for other reasons. By making substantive payments, a parent not only provides financial assistance but also maintains a sense of parental responsibility and connection to the children. So unless a parent is unable to work due to poor health or for other legitimate reasons, the noncustodial parent should pay meaningful child support.

Even in those rare instances when the custodial parent alone can pay the children's expenses, a court will expect the other parent to contribute. Children's expenses are the responsibility of both parents—regardless of their incomes.

4. *Relative parental expenses.* Before making decisions on child support, estimate your expenses after divorce. Appendix Two, the income and expense chart, may help. (I recommend that you make several copies of the chart so that you can mark it up freely.)

First, list all your expected income after your divorce (not including child support or alimony from this divorce), less any required deductions, such as taxes and Social Security. Second, estimate your average monthly expenses after divorce. (Review your checkbook for a year looking for any categories of expenses not listed on the chart, and add them.)

Note that you're asked to list all expenditures "needed" by you and your children. Start by listing all reasonable expenses, not just the bare necessities, keeping in mind that the "needs" of children whose parents jointly earn $150,000 annually are greater than for those children whose parents' income is $50,000.

Third, list any monthly unsecured debts (credit cards, student loans, debts to relatives) that you will be paying after your divorce. Finally, add up all the expenses and subtract them from your net income. The remainder is what's available for—or what's needed for—child support, alimony, or both.

You'll want accurate numbers, based on actual expenses, for discussions on support. Whether you'll be paying or receiving support, firm figures—not estimates pulled out of the air—are necessary to calculate what you need or what you can afford to pay. And your spouse will be more sympathetic to your arguments if they're based on verifiable numbers.

Allowing for Later Changes in Income

"We've agreed on $650 a month in child support based on Steve's present earnings," one mother pointed out. "But what if his income increases? Will the child support increase?"

When parental incomes rise or drop significantly, you can return to court to change the amount of child support, but there are drawbacks to doing so. You'll probably have little hard information about your ex-spouse's current income; also, returning to court is expensive.

You can remedy the first problem by requiring the paying parent (or both parents if appropriate) to provide the other with copies of income or tax records each year.

To avoid the expense of returning to court, you might formally agree to mediate future disputes regarding your children before resorting to litigation. Some couples agree to review child support annually in mediation.

My clients often ask to have the amount of child support change automatically as their incomes rise or fall. Ask your mediator or attorney whether your state law allows for such automatic adjustments—it probably doesn't. Defining income can be tricky, and most courts aren't willing to order changes in child support based on numbers that may be difficult to ascertain in the future.

You may also wonder if you need to bother changing your order. Can't you just informally agree to a change in the support amount? That's risky. If one parent pays less child support because the other agreed to an informal reduction, he runs the risk that she will later change her mind and sue him for the unpaid amounts. And she may well prevail.

If you're the parent receiving child support and the other parent informally agrees to pay more than ordered, he may later decide to count those extra amounts as credits against future payments, thus allowing him to quit paying child support for some period.

These risks are real. You're better off spending a few hundred dollars having your agreement formalized in a new court order.

What About Other Support Issues?

Besides monthly child support, other issues are important to your children's future financial care.

1. *Medical and dental insurance.* Who's going to carry this expense? Clients sometimes think that the parent whose employer provides the insurance should pay for it. Not necessarily. Even if the cost is withheld from that parent's paycheck, the other parent may partially or completely reimburse the paying parent. In my state, the parent paying child support is expected also to pay the cost of health insurance, even if the other parent is carrying it at her work.

2. *Uninsured medical and dental expenses.* There are three kinds of uninsured health expenses: (1) deductibles and copayments, (2) anything not covered by your policy, and (3) anything that exceeds the dollar limits of your policy. Be sure your order specifies how much of these expenses each of you is to pay.

3. *Life insurance*. You'll probably want to require that each of you maintain life insurance so that if one of you dies, the other has funds with which to raise your children. This requirement is particularly important for the higher-earning spouse—usually the one paying support.

Should the beneficiary of your insurance be the other parent, the children, or a trustee for the children? If the other parent is the named beneficiary, there will be no legal constraints on how the money is used. Some people are uncomfortable giving their ex-spouses such unbridled discretion.

If you name your children as beneficiaries, their other parent will, as guardian, handle the funds for them until they're eighteen, when they'll be legally entitled to receive the proceeds outright. Until that time, the surviving parent may use the money to pay the children's expenses.

The insurance company might, however, refuse to pay the benefits until the children are eighteen, thereby making those funds unavailable while the children are minors. If you're interested in naming your children as beneficiaries, ask your insurance agent when the money would be paid to them or their guardian.

Setting up a trust in your will is probably the best solution. If you name your estate as beneficiary of the insurance proceeds, those benefits will be paid to the executor of your estate, who will turn them over to the trustee of the trust you create in your will. When you draft your will, you can decide how those funds shall be distributed by the trustee and at what age your children should receive their shares outright. You can also decide, and state in your will, who will be trustee and manage those funds for your children. The trustee can be their other parent, or it can be anyone else you choose, such as your parents or siblings. The trustee's investments and expenditures for the children will be monitored by the court. If you're interested in setting up such a trust, talk to your lawyer about it.

4. *Making child support an obligation of the payor's estate*. If the parent paying child support dies without adequate insurance to con-

tinue it, the estate will be obligated to pay child support out of the remaining assets—if your divorce decree says so. Ask your attorney about this requirement.

5.   *College*. Your children's college expenses aren't always covered in support orders. If you want them to be, ask your lawyer about your legal rights in this area and raise the subject in mediation.

Who Makes Decisions About Your Children's Future Care?

State law grants each of you the right to make certain decisions regarding your children—for example, their education, medical care, religious affiliation, and discipline. Some rights are given to both parents; others may be given to just one of you or may be exercised only by your agreement.

For example, under Texas law the mother and father both have the right, after divorce, to make routine and emergency medical decisions for their child without conferring with the other. But what if the decision is neither routine nor an emergency? What if one parent wants his daughter to have braces or see a counselor and the other doesn't agree? You must choose at divorce how you will make such future decisions.

- Will both parents be free to make certain decisions without the other's concurrence? (For example, either parent can choose a counselor for the child without the other's agreement.)

- Will only the mother or only the father be entitled to decide? (For example, the father might make all educational decisions, and the mother might handle any investments in the children's names.)

- Will some decisions be made only by agreement? (Neither parent, for example, could enroll a child in an extracurricular activity without the other's consent.)

Each state defines parental rights differently, so ask your lawyer what rights are available to you and what your options are for exercising them.

If you're interested in joint decision making (meaning that you both must agree on decisions), consider whether this is workable in the years ahead. Many divorcing couples are comfortable making joint decisions for their children; their marital problems, whatever they've been, don't interfere with their parenting. The conflicts of other couples, however, spill over into their parenting styles. With such couples, joint decision making is an invitation to future frustration, if not catastrophe. They continue to quarrel over these choices, making themselves and their children miserable.

One parent, perhaps bitter over the divorce, may use joint decision making to maintain control over the other. When decision making is shared, one parent must obtain the other's consent before changing doctors, seeking counseling for a child, or enrolling the child in a school or extracurricular program—situations ripe for conflict if the couple engages in power struggles.

Some decisions, such as consenting to underage marriage, may never come up; but others, like those regarding education and medical care, may arise frequently. In these cases, plan to make decisions jointly only if you're sure you can do so cooperatively.

If you're not comfortable sharing decision-making authority, consider giving each of you a separate sphere of authority. For example, one of you might make medical decisions and the other make legal decisions.

What If Either of You Violates Your Agreement?

As the two of you plan your children's future care, your mediator and attorneys will want to be sure that your agreement has "teeth." This means that if one of you doesn't do what you're supposed to, the other has effective legal recourse. It could be that one parent doesn't pay child support or allow the other to have the children as ordered. Or one lets the health insurance lapse or changes a child's school without notifying the other.

The whole point of having a legal agreement is that it's binding—you both must comply with it unless you agree otherwise. If your paperwork is not legally binding, it's no more than a wish list. Therefore, your attorneys will be looking carefully at the language of your agreement to identify anything that might jeopardize its "enforceability." They want to be sure that, if your spouse violates the terms of your agreement, he can be held "in contempt"—meaning that he can be jailed or fined. Certainly most parents don't want the other jailed, but such remedies, though rarely used, motivate the parties to honor their divorce agreements.

To be enforceable by contempt, your agreement must be crystal clear. No judge will send someone to jail if the language describing the obligation is ambiguous. Therefore it's important that an attorney draft the agreement to ensure that it's enforceable.

One way lawyers do this is by using language that's been tested and upheld in court. The creative agreements parents often reach in mediation, however, may require wording that's never been tested in court; therefore, it's particularly important to review the language of your agreement with your attorney and ask specifically about its enforceability.

Part IV

Financial Fairness

13

Analyzing Your Assets and Debts

Who gets the house? Do you have to give your spouse half of your retirement benefits? Who's going to pay all the debts? Does the property have to be divided 50–50?

In mediation you and your spouse will be deciding such questions as you sort out a fair way to divide your estate. Because you can't determine what's fair without a full understanding of your finances, we'll first analyze your assets and debts:

- What you own and what you owe

- Whether individual assets or debts belong solely to one of you or are to be divided between you

- How much everything is worth

In the next chapter, we'll consider your options for dividing it up.

What Do You Own and What Do You Owe?

You may wait until you meet with your lawyer or mediator to begin this analysis, but if you start on your own, you'll save time (and fees). Review this material first to understand what to ask and then, if your estate is complicated, use these experts to help you gather and organize information. (Address legal questions to your lawyer;

your mediator can also answer many of them, depending on her background and philosophy of mediation, but your lawyer should be your legal adviser.)

Ask your spouse to join you in analyzing your property before starting mediation. Often a client begins our first session by showing me his careful delineation of the couple's assets and debts. Frequently his spouse has never seen this information before.

Lists and charts do help me understand a couple's estate, but I think couples would do better to develop this material together. When one spouse has done all the work, the other is often suspicious of the numbers.

Vivien and Charlie illustrate the dynamics of this situation. Sitting down at the round oak table in my office, Charlie handed me his computer printout of their assets and debts.

"I think this covers everything we have," he explained.

I looked at Vivien. "Have you seen this list?"

She shook her head. "Not really."

I gave it to my secretary to copy.

"I tried to explain it to her at home, but she wasn't interested," Charlie commented irritably while we waited.

"Well, you went so fast I couldn't understand what you were saying!"

"I've tried before to talk to you about these things, and you never want to listen," Charlie complained.

"That's not true. I've tried to get you to explain our finances to me, but you make it so complicated that I can't follow you."

After a few moments of uncomfortable silence, Vivien added, "You've never really told me what we have. You've insisted on keeping control of everything, and I don't know whether to believe you now or not. How do I know this list is everything?"

If this exchange sounds like a dialogue from your own marriage, you may want to talk to each other clearly about money matters before coming to mediation. If you're the one who has handled your finances, ask your spouse for a time when the two of you can review your estate. When you do, be clear and direct; avoid condescension and obfuscation. Offer to provide records for your bank accounts, business, and credit cards.

Being open and clear about your finances will gain your spouse's trust and save time and money. If your spouse believes you're hiding something, you may spend a great deal of time with lawyers and your mediator trying to convince her that you've disclosed everything.

If you know little about your estate, ask questions and insist on clarity. If your spouse doesn't offer the documents you need to verify his accounting, ask for them. You may review them on your own or ask your lawyer to help you examine them.

Divorce means becoming economically independent. If you never developed financial skills but depended on your spouse to provide them, a good way to begin gaining those skills is by understanding your own estate.

Although jointly working up an inventory may take more time, it'll pay off in mediation because you'll both be familiar with your property and less suspicious of each another. Of course, there may be points on which you disagree. Simply note those for discussion later in mediation and continue to identify all the issues on which you do agree.

Here's how to make an inventory of all your property. Take a pad of paper and list everything you own, using the list that follows as a prompter. For the moment, don't worry about whether the asset was acquired before or after marriage, who paid for it, whose name it's in, or what it's worth.

1. Real property (houses and land, cemetery plots)

2. Vehicles (cars, boats, motorcycles, mobile homes, airplanes)

3. Life insurance with cash surrender value (whole life or universal life, not term insurance)

4. Employment benefits (401Ks, pensions, thrift plans, stock options, stock ownership plans, accumulated vacation leave,

commissions earned during marriage but not yet received, workers' compensation, disability benefits, earned bonuses)

5. Cash and bank accounts (savings, checking, IRAs, mutual funds, CDs, SEPs)

6. Household goods

7. Collections (guns, tools, jewelry, stamps, antiques, artwork)

8. Livestock, pets

9. Closely held business interests (sole proprietorships, professional practices, partnerships, joint ventures, other nonpublicly traded corporate business entities)

10. Stocks, bonds, other securities

11. Monies receivable (notes or other debts owed to you, tax refunds owing, royalties)

12. Club memberships

13. Electronics and computers

14. Frequent flyer mileage accounts

15. Miscellaneous (crops, intellectual property, licenses, loss carried forward for tax deductions, lawsuits against others)

If your spouse isn't helping you prepare your inventory and you aren't sure what property he owns (such as retirement benefits or bank accounts), ask him. If your spouse doesn't cooperate, list those assets you know about and enlist the help of your attorney or mediator to find out about the rest.

For most categories, include every item you can think of. For example, list each bank account and each piece of real property separately. However, when you get to household goods, you may not need such detail. If you and your spouse agree on who's getting what furnishings and the approximate value of each person's share, and if you can physically separate your possessions before finalizing your divorce, you needn't list every table and food processor. If you can't agree, however, or if it isn't feasible to move all the items out of the house before your divorce is final, make detailed lists of the household goods going to each person.

Next, list all your unsecured debts. (Your secured debts will be listed later with the assets securing them.) Include student loans, all credit card debts that you don't pay off monthly, and unsecured debts owed to a family member, physician, or anyone else. Don't worry at this point about who incurred the debts or when—just list them.

Now look at Appendix One to see how we'll use this information. This property chart is a handy way to analyze property and debts so that you can divide them reasonably. As you see, you should list every asset and determine its value and any debt against it. Next, list the unsecured debts. When that's done, you're ready to consider how to divide these assets and debts between the two of you.

I've included a blank copy of Appendix One for you to duplicate and use for your own analysis. The appendix includes different charts for community and separate property and debts, which I'll discuss next.

What Are Community and Separate Estates?

Most states distinguish between property purchased with the parties' earnings during marriage (usually called "community" or "marital" property) and property purchased before marriage or received as a gift or through inheritance (sometimes called "separate" property). Various states may define these two categories differently and even give them different names, but making a distinction between the two is important. The court usually divides only the assets acquired with your earnings during marriage (which I'll call "community" assets); it normally awards separate assets to the party who owns them, with no compensation to the other spouse.

Review your inventory with your attorney to decide which articles fit into each category. Again, each state's law is different, so let your attorney be your guide.

Your lawyer may point out other property rights, such as a "right of reimbursement." This right arises when, for example, a husband spends money he earned during marriage to make repairs and mortgage payments on a house he owned before marriage. At divorce he gets to keep the house because it's his separate property, but it's now worth more because community funds were spent improving it and servicing its debt. Should he reimburse his wife for the marital income used to improve and maintain his separate property? Or should she get part of the house's increased value?

What if a wife used $30,000 inherited from her mother to pay debts incurred during marriage? Should she get any of that money back? Each state answers these questions differently, so consult your lawyer if you think these issues may come up in your divorce.

Occasionally one spouse will have a "separate" debt. He may have incurred the debt before marriage or during marriage in such a way that the other spouse bears no responsibility for it. When one party agrees to take over a community debt, he is entitled to receive community property of equal value as compensation; if the debt is separate, however, no compensating property is awarded to that spouse. Recognizing this distinction makes a difference in how you divide your assets. Only your lawyer can tell you if any of your debts are separate. Ask him.

What's It All Worth?

If you've listed all your assets and debts on the chart and have distinguished community and separate property and debts, your next task is to assign values.

Sometimes couples ask whether to use current values or those at the time of their separation, which may have been months or even years earlier. The answer varies from state to state, so ask your lawyer.

I'll review my earlier list of property categories, sharing thoughts about valuing property in each. Keep in mind that your lawyer can provide more specific information about how the courts in your state value property.

Real Property

Are you going to sell your house, or is one of you going to keep it? If you agree to sell your house and split the proceeds, you needn't give it a value on the chart. Just state in your paperwork that you'll remain joint owners and describe how you'll divide the net proceeds at sale—for example, 50–50 or 60–40.

You'll also want to state who will do the following:

- Live in the house

- Make the mortgage payments

- Pay for repairs and maintenance

- Decide the terms of sale

- Get the tax write-offs

These rights and obligations can be divided up any way you choose. Sally may live in the house and get the tax write-offs, while Chip pays half the cost of the mortgage and repairs in return for getting his share of the equity upon sale.

If you remain joint owners, do you need to sell the house immediately or postpone your divorce until the house is sold? Neither. You can put it on the market immediately or stay joint owners for years, sharing the proceeds when the house does sell.

Couples sometimes choose this arrangement when one parent wants to stay in the house until their children finish school but can't afford to buy the other out. Of course, the other parent must be willing to keep his or her funds tied up in the house during that time. It's a good idea to name a date after which either of you can insist on selling the house, so that you don't tie up your funds indefinitely.

If you want to stay joint owners, you'll need to decide how to divide the net proceeds at sale. Should you base each person's share on the value of the house at the date of separation, date of divorce, or date of sale?

For example, Ted and Margaret decide to stay joint owners of their home, valued at $150,000 with an $80,000 debt. Margaret plans to remain in the home and make all the mortgage payments. She and Ted decide to split their estate 60–40 in favor of Margaret and want to do the same with the proceeds from the eventual sale of the house.

But what if the house sells seven years later for $180,000, when the debt has been reduced to $70,000? Should Ted receive 40 percent of the equity at sale ($44,000) or 40 percent of the equity at divorce ($28,000)? If Ted agrees to the lower figure, he gets no return on his investment; his $28,000 share has earned no interest. On the other hand, Margaret may feel that he's not entitled to 40 percent of the higher figure because she'll be making the mortgage payments and thereby reducing the debt.

If Ted and Margaret decide instead that she'll buy him out of the house at divorce, she would put a net value of $70,000 in her column on the chart and agree to compensate Ted with additional property so that he'll still receive 40 percent of their estate.

If you don't agree on the value of your house, hire a realtor or an appraiser to give you an estimate. (I have found that a realtor is usually less expensive and does at least as good a job.) If you and your spouse have trouble agreeing on a realtor or appraiser, you might each choose one and then average their estimates.

Once you've placed a value for your house on the property chart, determine the balance on your mortgage (the principal amount owing, according to your mortgage holder) and enter that amount in the appropriate space. After subtracting the mortgage balance from the market value, put what's left—the equity—under "Net Value."

On the chart that is filled out as an example, note that the couple's house is worth less than the amount owed on the mortgage, which results in a negative value of $20,000. If you live in an area with declining real estate values, this result is an unfortunate possibility.

In determining your house's equity, you may want to consider the closing costs—realtors' and lawyers' fees and finance charges due at sale. Your lawyer can advise you whether judges in your area subtract these costs from the house's equity. If so, the person taking the house will have the advantage of putting a smaller number in his or her column.

For example, let's say that you are going to keep your house after divorce. It's worth $200,000 and has a mortgage balance of $150,000, making your equity $50,000. That means you must put $50,000 in your column and give your spouse $50,000 of some other asset as compensation. But if closing costs of $20,000 are subtracted from your home's equity, the net value in your column is only $30,000, meaning your spouse is entitled to $30,000 (not $50,000) in compensation.

Sometimes, when one party keeps the house and market prices are increasing, the other feels that the house should be valued with the rising market in mind. However, properties aren't valued by their possible future worth—they could, after all, decline rather than rise in value. Only current market value is considered.

Vehicles

You can usually value your cars and boats by referring to a "Blue Book," which gives three values for each vehicle: loan, retail, and trade-in. It probably doesn't matter which you use—just be sure to value all your vehicles the same way. Remember to add and subtract the recommended amounts for added features and unusual conditions. If you're not sure of your vehicle's value because it's damaged, talk to a dealer about it.

Next, determine the amount owing on any vehicle loan by asking the financing company. That figure is *not* the amount of your monthly payment multiplied by the number of months remaining on your note, because your payments include interest. The loan balance is the principal amount owing; your creditor can tell you how much that is. Enter this amount on the property chart next to the value of the vehicle. Then calculate the equity and enter it under "Net Value."

Life Insurance

Term life insurance has no market value, and most people carry only this kind. But whole life and universal life insurance policies do have value; if you have this kind of insurance, ask your agent to tell you its current cash surrender value. If you've borrowed against your life insurance, show the amount you owe and then enter the net value.

Employment Benefits

Employment benefits can be very easy or very difficult to evaluate. Let's look first at the easy ones.

Thrift plans, 401Ks, employee stock option plans, and other retirement plans to which you or your employer (or both of you) contribute are worth exactly the amount of the contributions plus earned interest. In legal parlance, these are known as "defined contribution plans." They're like bank accounts, and their value is easily determined. Your employer can tell you their current value.

"Pension" plans, also known as "defined benefit plans," are harder to evaluate. In this type of plan, your employer promises to pay you a pension in monthly installments when you retire, the amount of the payment depending on your highest years' earnings. It's difficult to determine the present value of these future payments for many reasons:

- You may not stay employed long enough to qualify for retirement.

- You don't know how long you'll live and therefore how many payments you'll receive.

- Not knowing what your highest years' earnings will be, you don't know how much the payments will be when and if you do receive them.

Nevertheless, actuaries can take a pretty good shot at evaluating these benefits. They use actuarial tables to determine how long you'll probably live; they look at how much you'd be entitled to receive per month if you could retire now and did so; and they calculate how much money it would take, if invested today, to make those monthly payments to you. With these sophisticated calculations, they can estimate the present market value of your expected future payments. Their estimate is, however, only that; it's based on probabilities. If you die tomorrow, the estimate is meaningless.

Also consider whether any of your employee benefits are separate property. Often a spouse began accumulating benefits before marriage, creating an asset that's part separate and part community property. Only the community portion—that earned during the marriage—is subject to division at divorce. Determining the value of each portion can be tricky; ask your attorney how it's done in your state.

The appraisal of your pension benefits should also not include any value accumulated *after* divorce. However, actuarial calculations may make certain assumptions about what may happen later, such as that you'll continue working at the same job (even though you may not). These assumptions affect the estimated value of your benefits. States vary as to what assumptions they allow in these calculations, so check with your lawyer.

Because the value of these assets is so uncertain, many couples decide to divide them—giving each spouse a percentage of the community portion. If you do this, each of you will receive your share of the monthly payments when the employed spouse retires. Thus you share any risks as to their future worth.

Sometimes, however, parties feel strongly about keeping all their retirement. You're not required to divide the community retirement benefits if the person keeping them can buy out the other's interest. But she may have nothing of comparable value to swap, because retirement benefits are often the most valuable asset in the marriage.

Whether or not you're the spouse who earned the benefits, you may not want to give up your share. Those monthly benefits may be important to you in the years to come. Or, if the benefit is a defined contribution plan (401K type) and your share can be paid to you as a lump sum, you may want to invest that sum and make it the basis of your own retirement.

If you receive a lump-sum payment for your share of your spouse's retirement benefits, you can roll it over into an IRA; indeed, if you don't you will have to pay tax on it and possibly a penalty as well. Be sure to ask a CPA how to handle these funds *before* you withdraw or transfer them.

In the next chapter, I discuss the possibility of two working spouses retaining their own retirement benefits as an even swap—and the dangers of doing so.

Other employee benefits, such as stock options and commissions due, can be very difficult to evaluate. Review them with your lawyer to find out how judges in your area normally value them.

Bank Accounts and Cash

These assets are worth exactly the amounts in the accounts. The only complication arises when accounts hold both community and separate property. If you created an account before you married or with other separate funds and later added community money, you may have difficulty calculating how much of each type remains in the account. Your lawyer can explain how courts do it in your state.

Household Goods

Unfortunately, most household goods are not worth what you paid for them: they depreciate quickly and dramatically. Their value at divorce, like that of all other assets, is what you can sell them for. That sofa you bought for $1,000 might bring only $100 at a garage sale or from a used furniture dealer—maybe a little more if you advertise it. Because these items are often not valuable, you can spend more than they're worth in mediators' and attorneys' fees by arguing about them.

To avoid this expense, you might try this approach. Each of you lists what you want; put values on the items on your list and on those remaining for your spouse. When you compare your lists, you'll probably find that each of you left out things the other re-membered, that you both want certain items and neither of you wants others, and that you disagree on some of the values.

Next, negotiate. If no one wants some items, have a garage sale and split the proceeds. As for what's left, try to agree on who gets what and fair values for each person's aggregate share.

If you agree that your two lists are fairly equal in value, you don't need to calculate aggregate values—just put "½" on the property chart under each person's column for household goods. But if one of you is getting more than the other, estimate a fair value for each share. If you can't, you'll need to evaluate every item. If you don't know how to value these assets, check with used furniture dealers, who for a modest fee will price your household goods.

If you owe a debt on any of these items, enter the balance owing next to the market value on the chart and then calculate the net value.

Collections

Experts can also evaluate your collections—guns, jewelry, or other items. Some, such as antiques and rare stamps, appreciate. Others, such as tools and jewelry, are usually not worth what you paid for them. A jeweler, for example, will probably give about 25 percent of what you paid for an item. You might get closer to half if you advertise it.

Livestock and Pets

I've never known a couple to put a value on their pets, though they've had strong disagreements over who should get them.

Livestock, on the other hand, can be valued like any other asset. Just find a competent appraiser.

Closely Held Businesses

If one of you owns an interest in a small business such as a family corporation, a dental practice, or a partnership, you'll need your attorney and CPA to determine its value.

Often the spouse who has run the business will say, "Well, if my wife thinks it's worth so much, she can take it for that amount!" Although this suggestion may sound fair on its face, it's rarely a sensible solution to valuation difficulties. A spouse who's not knowledgeable about the business or competent to run it is in no position to take it over, and her lack of desire to do so has nothing to do with its value. CPAs and business appraisers can provide reliable business valuations.

Being candid and cooperative is the least expensive route to valuing a business. Trying to deceive your spouse by hiding information about your business will only drive up the cost of your divorce. Your spouse's lawyer will file motions and have hearings and very likely get all the information she wants in the end. And a judge is likely to be unsympathetic to a party who has tried to hide assets. In fact, a judge may punish such behavior by requiring the offender to pay his spouse's legal fees.

Once you have given them your business records, the financial experts may apply several valuation methods to compute a fair market value. If they consider only the value of the assets (such as furniture, accounts receivable, and equipment) and subtract any debts owing, they'll get the "book value," usually the lowest value possible.

When Eddy and Caroline came in to mediate their divorce, Eddy's auto repair shop had about $150,000 in equipment and accounts receivable, but he owed $100,000 to the bank for the equipment. That made the *book value* of the business $50,000.

However, they could also evaluate Eddy's shop on the basis of its earnings. After expenses (including salaries), the business earned

$75,000 a year. A reasonable investor might pay $375,000 for a business that earns that much income. At that price, the business would pay for itself in five years.

Of course, whether a business can be sold at all may be in question. If it's a sole proprietorship and totally dependent on the reputation of the owner, perhaps no one would pay much for it.

Business appraisers take all these factors into account when estimating current market value. The divorcing parties may disagree on the validity of the resulting figure, but once they have numbers to work with, they can probably, with the mediator's help, agree on a value.

Eddy and Caroline met with a CPA they had jointly selected to evaluate the repair shop. After they talked to her about the financial details of their business, she talked to other professionals, gathered information about valuing auto repair shops in our area, ran the numbers, and came up with a reasonable value. Eddy and Caroline both felt comfortable with her analysis.

Stocks, Bonds and Other Securities

If you own publicly traded stock, you should have no difficulty obtaining values for these assets from a reputable stockbroker. However, because stock prices change daily, you'll need to select a day on which the value is to be fixed. You'll want a date early enough before the divorce that you have time to make the calculations necessary for completing Appendix One. After all, you may be unable to decide how to divide your property until you know the values for all your assets, including your stock.

On the other hand, if your stock is in a small, private corporation, it will probably be valued in the same way as family businesses are valued, as I discussed previously.

Monies Receivable

When valuing a debt owed to you, only the principal amount owing is considered, not interest. If the amount owing is uncertain, as a tax refund may be, you can agree to split the payment when you receive it. Other amounts receivable may be hard to evaluate because you don't know if you'll ever receive them—for example, the $5,000 you loaned your little brother when he was in trouble. He promised to pay you back, but that was three years ago, and his prospects still aren't good. Again, you may want to agree to split any funds you actually receive.

Club Memberships

These assets are hard to value if they're difficult to sell or can't be sold at all. The party keeping the membership is likely to claim it's worth little, and the other may put an unrealistically high value on it.

The following example illustrates one way to break an impasse. Greg wanted the tennis club membership but agreed that Alice could have it if she put it in her column at $10,000. Will she agree to take it for that? She might, or she might put it back in Greg's column for the same amount.

Electronics and Computers

I mention these items so that you won't forget them. Like other household or business goods, they depreciate quickly. You can probably get values by checking the classified ads or calling dealers.

Frequent Flyer Mileage Accounts

This asset is cropping up more often in divorce proceedings. Is the value of frequent flyer miles equal to the cost of purchased tickets for the same mileage? Your lawyer should advise you on how courts in your area value these accounts.

———

Now that you've done the groundwork—listing and valuing all your assets and debts and deciding which are community property and which separate—you're ready to think about dividing them fairly.

14

Dividing It All Up

Now that you've pulled your numbers together and know exactly what you own and how much you owe, we can consider your options for dividing your estate. We'll look at the following points:

- What portion you each get

- What items you each get

- What you'll need after divorce

How Much Do You Each Get?

It depends. Do you want to divide your property as a judge would? Or do you want to divide it according to what you think is fair?

In some states, a judge is required to divide property evenly; in others, she has the power to divide the marital estate unevenly if she thinks that's fair. (When a judge is required to divide property evenly, she may use alimony to help a lower-earning spouse.)

When dividing property unequally, a judge traditionally considers several factors. One spouse may, for example, receive more of the estate if her earning ability is limited by poor health, age, or the need to raise children. A judge may also award more property to one spouse when the other is at fault in the break-up of the marriage, earns more, has or expects to inherit a large separate estate, or has wasted community assets. Your lawyer can tell you how a judge in your area would probably divide your community estate. However, if you and your spouse are in agreement, you don't have to divide your estate as a judge would; you can do whatever the two of you believe is fair.

How do you determine what's fair? Deciding whether any of the just mentioned considerations apply to you is not a bad starting point.

•   "Fault" is a difficult issue to sort out in mediation, as each party may feel that the other bears responsibility for the failed marriage. Indeed, insisting on assigning blame can prevent you from achieving the important goal of mediation—preserving both parties' dignity, self-respect, and ability to coparent effectively.

•   The economic consequences of divorce are, however, another matter. Most couples recognize that dissolving their marriage may be financially devastating to one spouse or the other, usually the wife. National statistics show that men rebound financially rather quickly from divorce, whereas women—particularly those caring for children—tend to lose ground economically.

One spouse may have taken care of the children and maintained the home while the other earned most of the income. The former made a valuable contribution to the marriage but suffered a loss in wage-earning ability—while the other increased his value in the job market. Would it be fair for these people to divide their property equally with no compensation to the homemaker in the form of alimony or additional property (or both)?

The sizes of your community and separate estates may also affect how you divide your property. The smaller the community estate, the greater the disproportion needed to make a significant difference; a spouse's receiving 10 percent more property than the other doesn't mean as much when the estate is small.

• If one of you has or is expecting a large inheritance and the other has no such cushion, it may be fair to consider this when dividing the community estate.

• Has one of you wasted large amounts of community funds by gambling or spending money frivolously or improperly (on a lover, perhaps)? In one case I recently mediated, a husband put $40,000 into a trust fund for his children without telling his wife. Although the transfer of funds was not frivolous, the wife considered it improper because $20,000 (her share of those community funds) had been taken from her without her consent. If one spouse has been financially harmed by the other's unwarranted expenditures, the injured spouse might ask for more property as compensation.

Other considerations may also be relevant in determining your property division. Will one of you be less able to earn income after divorce because of child rearing responsibilities? Does poor health or age prevent one spouse from earning a reasonable living, whereas the other is healthy and has earning power? Would it be fair to divide property evenly under these circumstances?

Taking these considerations into account, you and your spouse must decide whether to divide your estate 50–50 or unevenly. When you've made that decision, enter the percentage to each of you on the lines in the bottom right-hand corner of the first page of Appendix One (the blank version, of course).

Who Gets What?

Once you've decided what portion of the estate each of you is to receive, it's time to decide which items you each get. Some items you probably know how to divide—for example, the wife will take her car and the husband will take his. For these items, place the net value amount in the appropriate spouse's column on the chart in Appendix One. The same may be the case for certain debts. If you're in agreement about who takes a particular debt, place the amount owing in the appropriate column.

How do you divide the remaining items according to the agreed-on percentages? Begin by discussing which assets each of you wants and why. For example, one of you may want to keep the house, or the other may want the art collection. Couples often discover during this conversation that they agree about how to divide most of their estate. Place the net values of those items on which you agree in the appropriate person's column.

You probably have some items left that you would both like to have—perhaps IRAs, cash, or retirement benefits. To decide how to divide these, add up how much each person already has, subtract each person's unsecured debts, and see how close you are to the agreed-on percentages.

For example, look at the first part of Appendix One to see how one couple worked out the division of their estate. Tom and Suzie initially agreed on everything except (1) whether she should receive any of his retirement benefits, (2) who should get the $5,000 in cash, and (3) who should pay their debts.

Once the figures were on paper, we could see that Suzie would have to take part of Tom's retirement in order to balance the negative equity she was receiving in the house. After some discussion, they decided on a 50–50 split of Tom's retirement benefits.

With that decision made, it was easier to discuss their cash and debts. We began by adding up how much each already had in his or her column. Tom had $36,000 (his car, household goods, life insurance, and half of his retirement), and Suzie had $28,000 (the house, half of Tom's retirement, and her car, household goods, retirement, and life insurance).

Because the total estate (after debts) was worth $64,000 and they had agreed that each should get half, Suzie needed another $4,000 from Tom. They might have transferred that value in several ways. Here are a few possibilities:

- Giving Suzie more of Tom's retirement in exchange for his getting some of the cash and less debt

- Giving Tom more cash and Suzie more household goods

- Giving Suzie all the cash and $1,000 of debt

- Giving Tom $1,000 in cash and all of the debts

Tom rejected the first option because he didn't want to give up more than half of his retirement. Suzie rejected the second because she didn't want more household goods. She also doubted she could pay off any of the debt with her lower salary. So they eventually decided to give Tom all the debts and a little of the cash.

Another possibility is to agree that one spouse will buy out the other's interest in the estate by making monthly payments. For example, Tom and Suzie could have agreed that Tom would keep his retirement and pay Suzie $25,000 over several years, payable in monthly installments, including interest.

The agreement would be formalized in a note secured by a document that would allow Suzie to seize property from Tom if he failed to pay. This arrangement would not have worked well for them, however. Tom had no property with which to secure a debt to Suzie, and he couldn't afford the payments on a $25,000 debt to her.

They could have sold their house and each paid half of the $20,000 owing on the mortgage at closing. In this scenario, Tom would be sharing the loss on the house, so Suzie would be entitled to less of his retirement or other assets. This possibility didn't appeal to Suzie and Tom, however, because they couldn't afford to come up with the balance owing on the mortgage and their closing costs.

The point is, no matter how complicated or simple your estate, the same procedures apply:

- List all assets and debts

- Determine values

- Decide on the percentage to go to each of you

- Divide up those items on which you agree

- Discuss ways to divide the remainder so that each of you gets the percentage to which you've agreed

Of course, you may find that one of you has so much in his or her column that there aren't enough items remaining to balance things out. If so, reconsider the division you've made and shift some items around.

Do You Really Need to Do All of This Analysis?

Some couples ignore all this calculating and just agree, for example, that the wife will take the house and that each will keep his or her own retirement benefits. If your estate is very simple and you already know its values, a division like this may be fair, and you can avoid going through the process described in the preceding section.

However, it is unwise to do this when you don't know precisely what you're giving up. Some couples announce to me that they've made such an agreement without first having determined the value of substantial assets, such as retirement benefits.

If a husband has been working for IBM for twenty years and his wife has been a school teacher for the same period but earned half his salary, her retirement benefits will be worth a great deal less than his. For him to keep his retirement benefits without providing a proper compensation to his wife would hardly be equitable. Some couples view retirement benefits as uniquely belonging to the spouse who earned them, but in actuality they're like a bank account or any other asset two people acquire during marriage.

Dividing Retirement Benefits

If you agree to divide retirement benefits earned by one of you, your mediator or lawyer will draft a special order called a Qualified Domestic Relations Order (QDRO, pronounced "quadro") to provide for this.

In the old days, there were no such orders. The divorce papers stated only that the wife (if the husband had earned the retirement) was entitled to receive her share of his retirement benefits "if, as, and when" he received them. The problem was that it was up to the husband to send his ex-wife her share—which he often failed to do. Therefore, the federal government created QDROs, which require employers to pay spouses their shares of the retirement directly. When the husband begins receiving his retirement benefits, the employer sends the wife her share by separate check.

Unfortunately, drafting QDROs is a chore for lawyers because every company's retirement plan is different—and the QDRO must be drafted to meet the unique specifications of each plan. For example, the order must state what will happen if one spouse dies before or after payments begin, and cover other details that vary from plan to plan. Therefore, be ready to discuss the QDRO with your mediator or lawyer (or both) and to pay an extra charge for its preparation.

Sometimes couples are hesitant to divide retirement benefits because they don't want to pay several hundred dollars to a lawyer to draft a QDRO. However, this reasoning is not sensible; the value of retirement benefits is probably far higher than the cost of preparing a QDRO. Some companies now provide master QDROs, which can save a good deal of drafting time and thus attorneys' fees—though your lawyers should carefully review these forms.

What Will You Need After Divorce?

As you prepare to discuss the division of your property, think carefully about your future economic needs. You don't want to negotiate your property division without first examining what your income and expenses will be after the divorce. That analysis may well influence what you're willing to settle for in your property division.

Looking at Your Future Income and Expenses

If you didn't fill out Appendix Two while reading Chapter Twelve, "Planning Your Children's Future Care," look at it now. This chart helps you estimate your income and expenses after divorce.

List on the first page all income you anticipate receiving—whether as salary, interest, rental, or self-employment income. Then subtract all taxes and other required salary deductions, leaving your monthly net income.

On the second page, list every expense you can think of, averaged monthly. The list provided may help you remember some of your expenses, but may fail to include others. Review your checkbook for the last year to pick up any expense categories not listed. Add these to Section D, line 28. Some expenses—such as the cost of your children's summer camp or Christmas and birthday gifts—don't occur monthly, so divide your annual cost by twelve to get a monthly average.

Be as accurate as possible. The list won't be useful if your numbers aren't realistic. You may want to add a little—a fudge factor—to account for small items you may be forgetting.

If you plan to assume credit card or other unsecured debts (such as a student loan or debt to a relative) on which you'll be making monthly payments, list these debts and the monthly payments under Section E and put the total at line 26 of Section D. Now you're ready to total your expenses and subtract them from your income to see what's left.

This exercise should give you a good idea of how much property you can afford to relinquish and how much you'll need to keep, particularly in light of the following considerations.

Other Economic Considerations

Before concluding this economic analysis, consider other aspects of your future finances:

- *Retirement.* Is it wise to trade off retirement income for some other asset if you've no other source of income for your later years?

- *Social Security.* Check with the Social Security Administration to find out the amount of benefits to which you'll be entitled at retirement. (When you fill out their simple chart, they can tell you your present entitlement.) Would it make a difference if you stayed married a little longer? Is that possibility worth considering?

- *Military benefits.* If your spouse has medical or commissary benefits resulting from military duty, can you continue to enjoy those benefits after divorce? Would your right to benefits increase if you stayed married a short while longer?

- *Liquidity.* How important is it that you leave your divorce with cash—a fund from which you can draw in an emergency or to purchase items that you know you'll need in the near future, such as household goods or a new car?

- *Assumption of debt.* The lower-earning spouse is usually less capable of taking over debt payments. Keep in mind too that even though your divorce papers say that your former spouse is responsible for a certain debt, if she or he doesn't pay it, the creditor will pursue *you* for payment. Thus, if you don't trust your spouse to pay debts with your name on them, you may want to take them yourself rather than endanger your credit.

- *Providing security for debt.* In some situations the spouse assuming a debt can provide security to the other by giving him or her a lien on property. For example, if the wife is keeping the family residence and the husband's name is on the mortgage she's responsible for paying, a deed of trust can be executed that allows the husband to take back the house if she defaults on making payments.

Similarly, if you've agreed that one of you will pay money to the other over time, the one doing so can sign a note for the amount owed. That debt can be secured with a deed of trust or other document that gives the other spouse the right to seize property if the debt isn't paid.

• *Tax consequences.* Consult a CPA about the tax consequences of any division of property you're considering. Pertinent questions might include the following:

> What are the tax advantages and disadvantages of keeping the house or other major asset? (Capital gains tax? Tax write-offs?) Are any of your assets taxable and therefore worth less than you thought (for example, your house, rental properties, retirement benefits, and stock)?
>
> How should you report and pay federal income taxes for the year of divorce?
>
> If your spouse didn't fully report income for prior years, can you protect yourself from tax liability for those arrearages?
>
> Which of you benefits more from the tax exemptions for your dependent children?
>
> What are the tax advantages and disadvantages of child support, alimony, and property transfers?

All of these concerns should be aired with your lawyer and any tax experts she recommends. The more fully you explore the financial implications of a possible agreement, the better prepared you'll be to make reasonable final decisions.

15

What About Alimony?

Alimony can be a painful subject. The person paying it often feels resentful, and the spouse receiving it may feel embarrassed. In this chapter I'll explore the following subjects:

- Why alimony came about and is still used in many divorces

- Whether alimony might be appropriate in your divorce

- How much you can afford to pay or need to receive

- What's fair

- How the payments affect your taxes

- How alimony is different from a property division

Why Alimony?

As I discussed with Laura and Patrick the terms of their divorce, I asked if they'd talked about alimony. Laura looked down at the table; Patrick grimaced.

"Why alimony?" he asked. "I've agreed to pay child support, but I don't see why I should pay anything for Laura's support. She can work."

Patrick's question is a good one, but complicated to answer. First, let's consider how alimony came about and whether it's now an anachronism.

Where Did It Come From?

In the old days, women stayed home, kept house, and raised children while men earned the family living. That was the implicit bargain most couples made when they married: women would be financially supported in return for their services as mothers and homemakers.

The advantage for a wife was that she could, supposedly, count on support for the rest of her life in return for working without pay as a homemaker and mother. The advantage for a husband was that he could, supposedly, count on the pleasures of a home and family while concentrating on earning income.

This bargain didn't always pan out. Sometimes a wife was a lousy mother or homemaker, and sometimes a husband failed to provide a living. And not everyone was happy with this preordained division of labor. Nevertheless, most people entering marriage understood the agreement, even if unspoken, and adhered to it.

Divorce was rare, but when it did occur, it usually left a wife far worse off economically than her husband. She may have lived up to her end of the bargain by raising children and maintaining a home, but she now found herself without the lifetime support on which she had counted.

A divorcing wife—faced with supporting herself and possibly her children—had dim prospects. Most women were not educated or trained for competing in the job market; those who were had probably been away from the business world for years and had lost their ability to compete. For those women who *were* prepared to enter the labor market, few jobs available to women paid enough to support a single individual comfortably, much less a family. A divorcing husband, on the other hand, had probably enhanced his earning ability during marriage.

Alimony was created to correct these economic inequities at divorce and to compensate divorcing women for the loss of financial security they'd been promised. The partner who'd economically benefited from the marriage contract paid support to the partner harmed by its breach.

Is Alimony Outdated?

Some of the social framework from which alimony emerged is disappearing. For example, these days many men assume more child-care responsibilities. Some even sacrifice professional gain in order to spend more time at home. Increasingly, I see couples who have divided their child raising responsibilities fairly evenly.

Most wives now work outside the home, many at high-paying jobs formerly unavailable to women. Indeed, we now occasionally see a husband receive alimony when his wife has been the higher-earning spouse.

Other aspects of the old social framework remain in place, however. Women still are usually the primary caretakers of children and limit their employment opportunities to fulfill that responsibility. Most women still receive substantially lower pay than similarly qualified men. For decades, the average salary of women working full-time has remained less than 70 percent that of men working full-time, even though the educational level of the average working woman is higher than that of the average working man.

What About Future Child-Care Responsibilities?

Child-care responsibilities can also place one parent at an economic disadvantage. Nina and Alex faced such a disparity. Both were lawyers; both had worked during their marriage and earned good incomes. At divorce, they agreed that Alex would be the primary caretaker of the children; he'd pick them up after school and take them to their activities in the afternoons.

Alex thought he could do much of his work at home with his computer and thereby manage a more flexible schedule. But he also knew that by choosing this route he was limiting his income; he wouldn't make partner anytime soon.

Nina and Alex decided that alimony was an appropriate way to compensate Alex for losing income while he was taking care of their children. They'd already worked out how they would share their children's expenses, but child support doesn't compensate a parent for earnings lost due to child-care responsibilities.

What Does the Law Require?

Judges may order alimony when they think it's appropriate and when state law allows. In making that decision, they consider such factors as the following:

- Length of the marriage

- Relative earning abilities of the spouses

- Whether the couple has children, how old they are, and how much each parent contributed to their raising

- Ages of the spouses

- Mental and physical health of each party

- Marital misconduct of either spouse

- Fault in breaking up the marriage

- Fraud, violence, and wastage of marital assets

- How property was divided, and other financial resources of each spouse

- Contribution by one spouse to the other's education and earning ability

- Property brought to the marriage by each

- The homemaking contributions of the spouse seeking support

- The efforts of the spouse requesting maintenance to seek employment

Which of these factors will a judge in your area consider, and how much weight will he give each? It depends on your state law and local practice. In some states, alimony can be awarded only in long-term marriages; in others, it's available even in marriages of short duration. In some, the term for alimony may not exceed three years; in others, it's presumptively for life. Ask your attorney how alimony is handled in your state.

What's Fair?

Now it's time to grapple with the crucial question: is alimony appropriate in your case? Asking the following questions might help you decide.

Did one of you give up earning potential to maintain a home and family?

Will child-related duties after divorce limit either party's earning ability?

Will one of you suffer a reduction in living standards because of divorce?

How long have you been married? (Most of us recognize that one spouse has more residual responsibility to the other if their marriage lasted ten or twenty years rather than two.)

How well prepared is the lower-earning spouse to enter the job market? Does she need additional education to compete for jobs? How much time and expense will that education require?

Does either spouse have significant health problems that interfere with earning ability?

How Much Do You Need and What Can You Afford?

As the two of you mull over the questions just presented and sort
out whether alimony is appropriate in your case, you'll also want to
look realistically at your income and expenses. How much alimony
does the recipient need? How much can the other afford?

If you didn't review Appendix Two while reading Chapter Fourteen, "Dividing It All Up," do so now. In that chapter I discuss how
to use the chart in Appendix Two to analyze your financial needs
after divorce. Using this chart will help you decide how much alimony, if any, is appropriate and realistic for you and your spouse.

How Long Should It Last?

Couples usually limit alimony to the time needed for the recipient
to successfully reenter the job market, though in the case of long-
term marriages and older spouses, the payments may be for life.

You may want to lower the payments as the recipient's earning
ability improves. For example, Mark and Mary Ann agreed that he
would pay her $2,000 a month for two years; then, after she finished
school, the payments would drop to $1,000 a month for another two
years. By then, they reasoned, she should be able to support herself.
(You must be careful, however, not to reduce the payments in a way
that would invalidate them as alimony and cause the IRS to "re-
capture" them—causing the payor to pay tax on previously de-
ducted payments.

Many couples agree to terminate alimony when the recipient re-
marries, though such a provision seems to perpetuate questionable
notions of economic dependency. Should a wife be regarded as a financial liability to be shifted from one husband to another?

You can tie the end of alimony to other contingencies as well,
but be careful about those involving children. If you agree to end

alimony payments at the same time that child support would normally end, the IRS will consider the payments to be child support—causing you to lose the tax advantages (or disadvantages) of alimony.

For example, Ginny and Lou decided that Lou would pay $500 a month in child support and another $1,000 a month in alimony. So far so good. They then decided that the alimony payments would end at the same time as the child support payments—when their daughter turned eighteen. It now appears that Ginny and Lou are simply relabeling their child support as alimony so that Lou can deduct the payments. The IRS doesn't allow this sort of subterfuge and will consider these payments child support rather than alimony.

Alimony always ends on the death of the recipient spouse, and it's not transferable to anyone else.

What Are the Tax Consequences of Alimony?

Alimony payments are tax deductible for the paying party and must be reported as income by the receiving party. For this reason, alimony is a sensible way to shift income from the higher-earning spouse (who can use the deductions) to the lower-earning spouse (who's in a lower tax bracket).

Alimony provisions must be carefully drafted to achieve these ends. It's imperative that you have a CPA or tax attorney review your divorce papers to make sure that nothing in them will cause you tax problems later.

How Is Alimony Different from Property Division or Child Support?

The payment of money from one spouse to the other can be called alimony, a property transfer, or, in some cases, child support. For example, Mary Ann and Mark agreed that he would pay her $2,000 a month for two years and then $1,000 a month for another two years. They also agreed that Mark would pay an additional $1,200 a month in child support.

They could have labeled the $2,000 and $1,000 monthly payments as alimony or as part of Mary Ann's share of their marital property—or as additional child support. If they call the payments alimony, Mark can deduct them from his taxes, and Mary Ann will report them as income and pay tax on them. If they make the payments part of their property division, Mark can't deduct them, and Mary Ann won't have to report them as taxable income. If they call them additional child support, they're also tax-free income to Mary Ann and not deductible for Mark.

If they choose to describe the payments as Mary Ann's share of their marital property, Mark's obligation would normally be written up in a promissory note and secured by a lien on property he receives. If they're alimony, they're not secured in any way and may be harder to collect if not paid. Or, depending on state law and how the language is drafted, they may be enforceable by contempt—as are child support payments. (You may remember from Chapter Twelve, "Planning Your Children's Future Care," that contempt is a very strong remedy. It provides for fines and jail sentences for offending parties, though only at the other party's request.)

Discuss these various options with your lawyer to be sure you understand the legal advantages and disadvantages of each route.

Life Insurance

Alimony provisions usually require that the paying spouse maintain sufficient life insurance to continue the payments if he or she dies.

Other Forms of Payment

Sometimes parties decide that after divorce one will make certain payments—such as car or health insurance—for the other. These payments actually are alimony and should be identified as such in your divorce papers if you want the tax advantages of alimony.

You may, however, prefer to make the payments a set dollar amount every month rather than require one spouse to make car or insurance payments for the other. It's cleaner and simpler that way. Both of you know exactly how much the monthly payment will always be; it won't change depending on the amount of the car or insurance payments. And the spouse receiving alimony is in charge of making her own payments.

As you wrestle with the issue of spousal support, you may rely primarily on your state's guidelines or decide for yourselves what's fair. Most couples try to strike a balance between their legal requirements and their sense of equity.

Afterword

Divorce can be a time of transition, growth, and adjustment to new roles—or it can be a time of fighting and destruction. Mediation offers the healthier route: separation with dignity and respect. And it allows parents to restructure their lives in a way that is least stressful for their children.

For most couples, mediation is the most responsible, caring, and creative way to dissolve their marriage—and to address future issues regarding children and support as they arise.

For Further Reading

I have found almost all of these books at my local library, and many are also available at the bookstore. If you browse through your bookstore or library you will probably find additional, equally helpful books.

For Parents

Mom's House, Dad's House. Isolina Ricci. (Macmillan, 1980). An excellent, detailed, and practical guide that explains the emotions and issues of children in divorce. The author emphasizes the importance of both parents' making real homes for their children and focusing on parenting roles and their children's best interests. I wish I'd read this book twenty years ago when I was getting divorced. If you're going to read only one book on the subject, I recommend this one.

Healthy Divorce. Craig Everett and Sandra Volgy Everett. (Jossey-Bass, 1994). Both authors are therapists and have worked extensively with divorcing couples. Whereas other books listed here are solely about helping children with divorce, this one also provides a step-by-step examination of the entire divorce experience.

The authors take us from "Early Warning Signs" through "Living in a Blended Family Network," providing an excellent guide through the emotional and legal issues of divorce and its aftermath. They strongly recommend mediation and include advice on how to make the most of the mediation experience.

Vicki Lansky's Divorce Book for Parents. Vicki Lansky. (Signet, 1996). A very readable, comprehensive book. Detailed and age-specific information about how children react to divorce and how to make it easier for them.

What Every Child Would Like Parents to Know About Divorce. Lee Salk. (HarperCollins, 1978). A psychiatrist talks to parents about the emotional issues their children encounter when the parents divorce. Quite readable. I particularly liked his chapter "What to Tell Your Child"—excellent material to review before explaining to your children that you're divorcing.

Growing Up Divorced. Linda Francke. (Faucett, 1984). This book describes, by age group, the emotional issues children face when their parents divorce. Because children are very adept at hiding their feelings or often don't know how to express them, this guide provides valuable advice on helping your children understand divorce.

The Nurturing Father. Kyle D. Pruett. (Little, Brown, 1988). A child psychiatrist reports on his study of families in which fathers are the primary caretakers of young children. He found these children to be emotionally healthy and even precocious and concludes that they do especially well because *both* parents are strongly involved with their children—probably because mothers in these circumstances are often more involved than are fathers when mothers are the primary caretakers.

The Divorced Parent. Stephanie Marston. (Morrow, 1994). I liked best the chapters "Dealing with Difficult Exes," "Money," and "Building a Life of Your Own." Ms. Marston gives good and detailed advice on what you can do when your ex-spouse is impossible, how to handle money matters in your divorce and afterwards, and how to rebuild your life after divorce.

Second Chances: Men, Women and Children, a Decade After Divorce. Judith Wallerstein and Sandra Blakeslee. (Ticknor and Fields, 1989). The authors followed sixty families through divorce and the next ten to fifteen years to determine the long-range effects of divorce on parents and their children.

The result is a disturbing look at how long the dislocation and pain of divorce can last for both adults and children—particularly if the parents don't make every effort to recover from their anger and grief, get their lives back on track, protect their children from their anger and distrust, and help their children deal with the fear, anger, and confusion they experience. The authors clearly delineate the devastating effects on the children when either parent fails to stay fully involved in their lives and provide the continuing love and support the children need.

Who Will Take the Children? A New Custody Option for Divorcing Mothers and Fathers. Susan Meyers and Joan Lakin. (Bobbs-Merrill, 1983). If you're a mother and considering an agreement in which your children's father provides their primary care, you'll be interested in this account of other women who have made the same decision. According to the authors, the vast majority of these mothers believe they were better parents as a result of their decision and that it was best for them and their children. The authors also describe the social pressures on women making this choice and provide support for women who do.

For the Sake of the Children. Kris Kline and Stephen Pew (Prima Publishing, 1992). A mother who spent years in custody litigation writes about how to avoid her mistakes. I liked the advice about how to deal civilly with your former spouse, your children's new stepparent, your former in-laws, and your own mother. Although the authors focus on special occasions such as weddings, graduations, and birthdays, they also offer practical advice on dealing day-to-day with people with whom you may be angry but must nevertheless include in the lives of your children, for their sake. The authors' emphasis is on not damaging, and even fostering, your children's relationships with those family members you would just as soon never see again.

Sharing the Children. Robert E. Adler (Adler and Adler, 1988). Adler gives detailed and readable advice on how to work out a divorce with your spouse and build a workable relationship for co-parenting. He discusses how to handle your children's concerns, respond to your spouse's anger, manage your own fears, and cope with the legal system. A very good manual for any parent going through divorce.

Divorced Families: A Multidisciplinary Developmental View. Constance Ahrons. (Norton, 1987). The author categorizes divorcing couples in descending order as "perfect pals," "cooperative colleagues," "angry associates," and "fiery foes," with advice as to how to end up in the positive categories rather than the negative ones.

For Children

The age ranges I give for the children's books are rough guesses. I haven't had a young one in quite a few years, so your estimate will be better than mine.

Preschool

The Dinosaurs Divorce. Laurene and Marc Brown. (Little, Brown, 1986). My clients tell me that their kids love this book. Colorful cartoon dinosaurs address children's fears and concerns about divorce. The dinosaurs let kids know that it's OK to feel fear, anger, sadness, and relief, and that life gets better in time.

Sometimes a Family Has to Split Up. Jane Werner Watson (Crown Publishers, 1988). A well-told story with pleasant illustrations about a child whose parents quarrel and then decide to divorce. The book acknowledges the child's fear and confusion, tells of his parents' reassurances, and shows how his new life unfolds.

Two Homes to Live In: A Child's Eye View of Divorce. Barbara Shook Hazen. (Human Science Press, 1978). I like this depiction of a small child's experience of divorce—the sadness, the parental reassurances, and the acceptance. Good illustrations by Peggy Luks.

Please Come Home. Doris Sanford. (Multnomah Press, 1985). With lovely illustrations, this slender book tells the story of Jenny, whose parents are divorcing. Her teddy bear gives her wise advice, and she recovers from her sadness. For ages four to seven.

Elementary School

At Daddy's on Saturdays. Linda Walvoord Girard. (Albert Whitman and Co., 1987). Katie watches her dad move out; she feels sad, frightened, and finally reassured by his love, attention, and new home. A lovely book for five- to ten-year-olds.

When Mom and Dad Divorce. Stephen L. Nickman. (Julian Messner, 1986). An excellent book on divorce for eight- to twelve-year-olds. The author tells stories about children of divorcing parents and explores what they felt and how they managed.

When Your Parents Get a Divorce: A Kid's Journal. Ann Banks. (Puffin Books, 1990). This author takes the novel approach of creating a journal-notebook in which children can describe their feelings, draw pictures, and explore the dynamics of their family situation. I liked this book very much and would think a youngster would enjoy this approach. You'll need to get this one at a bookstore. For ages eight to fourteen.

The Facts About Divorce. Caroline Eversen Lazo. (Crestwood House, 1989). This little book can be read in less than an hour. It answers many questions children have about divorce and suggests what they can do to make the process easier on themselves. For ages ten to fifteen.

Everything You Need to Know About Your Parents' Divorce. Linda Carlson Johnson. (Rosen Publishing Group, 1993). A simple and easy-to-read explanation of divorce—what it means and how it affects children. For ages ten to thirteen.

Preteen and Teen

The Kids' Book of Divorce. The Unit at the Fayerweather Street School. (Lewis Publishing, 1981). A great introduction to divorce, written by children of divorced families. Twenty kids ages eleven to fourteen speak to their peers about divorce—what it means, how it feels, what you can and can't do about it. I liked this one best because it's probably the most approachable for kids this age.

How It Feels When Parents Divorce. Jill Krementz. (Knopf, 1984). Nineteen children ages seven to seventeen tell their stories. The kids talk about how it feels when parents fight and when they don't see one of their parents enough, and what it's like to have step-parents, new siblings, and two homes. They talk frankly about the pain of divorce, but they also talk about the good points: seeing more of their fathers than before, no longer witnessing their parents' fights, finding their parents more relaxed and fun to be with, and the pleasure of having new step- or half-siblings.

Your child will probably be reassured to hear that other children have been through the same experience and have adapted successfully to their parents' separation and divorce. It's also a good book to read yourself because it gives valuable insight into what children of divorcing parents feel, what matters to them and what does not.

It's Not the End of the World. Judy Blume. (Dell, 1972). If you're already a Judy Blume fan, you'll be glad to know that she's written this one on divorce. We empathize with twelve-year-old Karen Newman as she struggles with the confusion and anxiety caused by her parents' divorce. After several months of coming to terms with new family relationships, she accepts her new life; the book ends with her saying, "I had a B+ day today." Probably best for upper elementary and junior high kids.

The Boys and Girls Book About Divorce. Richard Gardner. (Bantam Books, 1970). This is a very popular book with youngsters. The author, a child psychiatrist, talks frankly to youngsters about divorce— their anger and that of their parents, how to tell whether parents love them, what it feels like when Dad doesn't show up on time or mother starts dating, and what they can and cannot do to make their situations better. The author even gives good advice on how to live with stepparents. An excellent guide for children eight to thirteen.

How to Get It Together When Your Parents Are Coming Apart. (McKay Co., 1976). Though a bit dated when it talks about legal matters, this book is refreshingly clear and direct without being condescending. It covers the emotional, logistical, and legal problems that both kids and their parents are likely to experience in divorce. It also suggests how adolescents can make their transition easier and lists sources for help. The author covers, very matter-of-factly, some of the reasons why parents divorce, from drifting apart, to other romantic interests, to homosexuality. I think the author's candid approach does a lot to demystify divorce for young people. Probably best for kids fourteen and older.

Surviving Your Parents' Divorce. Charles Boeckman. (Franklin Watts, 1980). An easy-to-read explanation of what divorce is all about, what a teenager can expect, and how to cope. It also covers stepfamilies. Probably best for ages thirteen to sixteen.

Coping When Your Family Falls Apart. Dianna Daniels Booher. (Julian Messner, 1979). The author covers the emotional game-playing in which parents and children often engage during the divorce, the emotions the youngster is likely to feel, coping devices, legal terminology, and stepfamilies. A good explanation for the teenager.

Appendix One

Property Chart

The first part of Appendix One (pp. 196–198) is a sample property chart for Tom and Suzie, whose mediation was discussed in Chapters Eight and Fourteen. Following this example are blank forms for you to copy and use.

Community Property

Property	Fair Market Value	Secured Debt Balance	Net Value	To Wife	To Husband
1. Residence	150,000	170,000	(20,000)	(20,000)	
2. W's car	10,000	11,000	(1,000)	(1,000)	
3. H's car	4,000	1,000	3,000		3,000
4. Household furnishings (See attachment.)	8,000	–0–	8,000	5,000	3,000
5. W's retirement	15,000	–0–	15,000	15,000	
6. H's retirement	50,000	–0–	50,000	25,000	25,000
7. H's life ins.	5,000	–0–	5,000		5,000
8. W's life ins.	4,000	–0–	4,000	4,000	
9. Cash	5,000	–0–	5,000	4,000	1,000
TOTAL:	251,000	182,000	69,000	32,000	37,000

Less Unsecured Community Debts:

Creditor	Balance	To Wife	To Husband
1. Mastercard	2,000		2,000
2. Visa	2,000		2,000
3. Sears	1,000		1,000
TOTAL:	5,000		5,000

NET COMMUNITY: $64,000   To wife: $32,000 (50 percent)

To husband: $32,000 (50 percent)

Separate Property

Husband's Separate Property

	Fair Market Property Value	Secured Debt Balance	Net Value
1. Rental house	100,000	80,000	20,000
TOTAL:	100,000	80,000	20,000

Husband's Separate Debts

Creditor	Debt Balance
1. Student loan	20,000
TOTAL:	20,000

Wife's Separate Property

	Fair Market Property Value	Secured Debt Balance	Net Value
1. Life insurance	5,000		5,000
TOTAL:	5,000		5,000

Wife's Separate Debts

Creditor	Debt Balance
1. Student loan	5,000
TOTAL:	5,000

Attachment to Appendix One:
Household Furnishings

Wife's Household Furnishings

1. Living room
   Couch, coffee table, two end tables, area rug, grandfather clock, three flower prints, bookshelf, books
2. Master bedroom
   Bed, two lamps, two nightstands, chest
3. Kitchen
   Daily flatware and dishes, food processor, blender, wine glasses, china, silver, candlesticks, crockery, refrigerator, washer and dryer, half of cooking utensils
4. Baths
   All accessories, towels, sheets, and other linens
5. Dining room
   Table and six chairs, chest, two prints
6. Other
   Vacuum cleaner, lawn equipment, all decorative pieces and artwork, camping equipment, half of family pictures

Husband's Household Furnishings

1. Living room
   VCR, hall tree, entertainment center, CD player
2. Guest bedroom
   Bed, chair, desk, area rug, two prints, chest
3. Kitchen
   Half of all cooking utensils, microwave
4. Study
   Computer and printer, desk, two chairs, framed pictures, couch, three tables, bookcases, books
5. Garage
   Tools, bike rack
6. Other
   Stamp and baseball card collections, half of family pictures

Community Property

Property	Fair Market Value	Secured Debt Balance	Net Value	To Wife	To Husband
1.					
2.					
3.					
4.					
5.					
6.					
7.					
8.					
9.					
10.					
11.					
12.					
TOTAL:			(1)_____	(2)_____	(3)_____

Less Unsecured Community Debts:

Creditor	Balance	To Wife	To Husband
1.			
2.			
3.			
4.			
5.			
6.			
7.			
8.			
9.			
TOTAL:	(4)_____	(5)_____	(6)_____

NET
COMMUNITY (1−4): $_____   To wife (2−5): $_____ (___ percent)

To husband (3−6): $_____ (___ percent)

Separate Property

Husband's Separate Property

	Fair Market Property Value	Secured Debt Balance	Net Value
1.			
2.			
3.			
4.			
5.			
TOTAL:			

Husband's Separate Debts

Creditor	Debt Balance
1.	
2.	
3.	
TOTAL:	

Wife's Separate Property

	Fair Market Property Value	Secured Debt Balance	Net Value
1.			
2.			
3.			
4.			
5.			
TOTAL:			

Wife's Separate Debts

Creditor	Debt Balance
1.	
2.	
3.	
TOTAL:	

Appendix Two

Income and Expense Form

A. Gross Earnings per Month:
   1. Gross wages and salary income   \$_____
   2. Commissions, tips, and bonuses   \$_____
   3. Self-employment income (net of expenses   \$_____
       other than depreciation and tax credits)
   4. Rental income (net of expenses other   \$_____
       than depreciation)
   5. All other income actually received (specify):   \$_____

   _____

   _____

      Gross Earnings per Month   \$_____ (A)

B. Actual Deductions per Month
   1. Income tax withholding   \$_____
   2. FICA (Social Security)   \$_____
   3. Health insurance   \$_____
   4. Union dues   \$_____
   5. Other deductions (specify)

   _____   \$_____
   _____   \$_____

      Total Actual Deductions per Month   \$_____ (B)

C. Net Money Actually Received per Month   \$_____ (C)
   Subtract (B) from (A)

D. Total Money Needed per Month by Me and Minor Child(ren) Living With Me. *(For items that are not paid monthly, express the amount as a monthly average.)*

    1. Rent or house payment $_____

    2. Real property taxes (omit if part of house payment) $_____

    3. Residence maint. (repairs, yard) $_____

    4. Insurance—home or renters (omit if part of house payment) $_____

    5. Utilities—gas $_____

    6. Utilities—electric and water $_____

    7. Telephone (incl. avg. long dist.) $_____

    8. Utilities—garbage service $_____

    9. Groceries and household items $_____

   10. Meals away from home $_____

   11. School lunches $_____

   12. Dental and orthodontia $_____

   13. Medical and prescriptions $_____

   14. Laundry and dry cleaning $_____

   15. Car payment $_____

   16. Gas and vehicle maintenance $_____

   17. Clothing $_____

   18. Insurance—car $_____

   19. Insurance—life $_____

   20. Insurance—health (omit if payroll deduction) $_____

   21. Child care $_____

   22. Children's activities $_____

   23. Entertainment $_____

   24. Haircuts $_____

   25. Cable TV and newspaper $_____

   26. Total monthly payments on debts (list below at E and show only total here) $_____

   27. Support or alimony payments to other persons (not this family) $_____

   28. Other (specify):

       Miscellaneous $_____

       Gifts $_____

       Vacations $_____

       Books and magazines $_____

       Children's summer camp $_____

       _____ $_____

       _____ $_____

       _____ $_____

Total Money Needed per Month $_____ (D)

E. Total Monthly Payments on Other Debts:

Description of Debt	Balance Now Owed	Date of Final Payment	Amount of Monthly Payments
(e.g., Visa)	$_____	_____	$_____
_____	$_____	_____	$_____
_____	$_____	_____	$_____
_____	$_____	_____	$_____
_____	$_____	_____	$_____
_____	$_____	_____	$_____
_____	$_____	_____	$_____

Total Monthly Payments on Debts $_____ (E)

F. Difference Between Money Received and Money Needed
Subtract (D) from (C) $_____ (F)

Appendix Three

Rules for Mediation

1. *Definition of mediation.* In mediation, an impartial person, the mediator, facilitates communication between the parties to promote settlement of a dispute between them. The mediator may suggest ways of resolving the dispute but may not impose her own judgment on the issues on behalf of the parties.

2. *Neutrality of the mediator.* The mediator shall not serve as a mediator in any dispute in which she has any financial or personal interest in the result of the mediation. Prior to accepting an appointment, the mediator shall disclose any circumstance likely to create a presumption of bias or to prevent a prompt meeting with the parties.

3. *Authority of mediator.* The mediator does not have the authority to decide any issue for the parties but will attempt to facilitate the voluntary resolution of the dispute by the parties. The mediator is authorized to conduct joint and separate meetings with the parties and to offer suggestions to assist the parties in achieving settlement. If necessary, the mediator may also obtain expert advice concerning technical aspects of the dispute, provided that the parties agree and assume the expenses of obtaining such advice. Arrangements for obtaining such advice shall be made by the mediator or the parties, as the mediator shall determine.

4. *Parties are responsible for negotiating their own settlement.* The parties understand that the mediator will not and cannot impose a settlement in their case. The mediator, as an advocate for settlement, will use every effort to facilitate the negotiations of the parties but does not warrant or represent that settlement will result from the mediation process.

5. *Decorum.* The parties shall treat each other and the mediator with consideration and good manners. They will not interrupt when another is speaking, will abstain from name calling and blaming, and will make every effort to conduct the mediation proceedings with respect for the other participants' feelings and rights of expression.

6. *Privacy.* Mediation sessions are private. The parties and their representatives may attend mediation sessions. Other persons may attend only with the permission of the parties and with the consent of the mediator.

7. *Confidentiality.* Confidential information disclosed to a mediator by the parties or by witnesses in the course of the mediation shall not be divulged by the mediator. All records, reports, or other documents received by a mediator while serving in that capacity shall be confidential. The mediator shall not be compelled to divulge such records or to testify in regard to the mediation in any adversary proceeding or judicial forum. Any party that violates this order shall pay all reasonable fees and expenses of the mediator and other parties, including reasonable attorneys' fees incurred in opposing the efforts to compel testimony or records from the mediator.

The parties shall maintain the confidentiality of the mediation and shall not rely on or introduce as evidence in any arbitral, judicial, or other proceeding: (1) views expressed or suggestions made by another party with respect to a possible settlement of the dispute; (2) admissions made by another party in the course of the mediation proceedings; (3) proposals made or views expressed by the mediator; or (4) the fact that another party had or had not indicated willingness to accept a proposal for settlement made by the mediator.

8.   *No stenographic record.* There shall be no stenographic record of the mediation process, and no person shall tape-record any portion of the mediation session.

9.   *No service of process at or near the site of the mediation.* No subpoenas, summons, complaints, citations, writs, or other process may be served upon any person at or near the site of any mediation session or upon any person entering, attending, or leaving the session.

10.   *Interpretation and application of rules.* The mediator shall interpret and apply these rules.

11.   *Fees and expenses.* The mediator's fee shall be borne equally by the parties unless they agree otherwise.

About the Author

PAULA JAMES is a family law attorney-mediator practicing in Austin, Texas. Having litigated divorces and other family law matters since 1981, Ms. James began mediating full-time in 1992.

Ms. James has recently served as chair of the Family Law Section of the Travis County Bar Association and as chair of the Family Law Subsection of the Travis County ADR (Mediation) Section. She has also created and chaired bar and other nonprofit efforts to provide free and low-cost legal assistance to low-income individuals. One, the Women's Advocacy Project, is a statewide nonprofit organization that has been providing low-cost legal services to indigent clients for thirteen years. Another, the Match Program, has been providing low-cost family law representation to low-income clients in Travis County since 1992.

Ms. James received a Ph.D. degree in English from Texas Christian University in 1972 and a J.D. degree from the University of Texas School of Law in 1976.

Index

Litigation: example of, 4–10; family
and social influences on, 122–123;
retainer fees in, 40, 49; versus
mediation, 3–4, 15, 60–61
Livestock as an asset, 161–162
Lying as an emotional problem,
108–109

M

Mediation, 3–28, 59–82, 205–207;
advantages of, 60–61; bringing
lawyers to, 24; clarifying goals in,
71; confidentiality in, 206–207;
considering options in, 80–81;
defined, 205; discussing with
spouse, 59–61; documents to bring
to, 66–67; example of, 10–15;
family and social influences against,
122–123; finalizing divorces in,
74–75; identifying issues in, 78;
individuals unsuited for, 25–26;
making agreements with spouses
before, 62–64; making appoint-
ments for, 64–66; making decisions
in, 81; with obstinate spouses,
22–24; preparing and filing legal
documents in, 72–74; privacy in,
61, 206; reaching agreements in,
77–82; revealing financial information in, 26–28, 62–64, 66–67, 78–
80; rules for, 70, 205–207; staying
on track in, 81–82; steps in, 69–75;
styles of, 31–33; tackling legal
issues in, 71–72; versus litigation,
3–4, 15, 60–61; and women as
caretakers, 20–22; and women as
negotiators, 17–20
Mediators, 29–46; authority of, 205;
clerics as, 34–35; experience of,
30; fees of, 38–40; finding, 35–38;
interviewing, 38; and knowledge
of family law, 30–31; neutrality of,
42–43, 205; overview of, 29; pre-
mediation conversations with, 65;
qualifications for, 29–31; role of,
41–46; styles of, 31–33; therapists
as, 33–34; training for, 29–30

Medical expenses, 141
Mental health professionals. *See*
Therapists
Military benefits, 173
Moneys receivable as assets, 163–164
Mutual respect as an emotional aid,
92

N

Needs: analyzing, 171–174, 202; con-
fessing, 95
Neutrality of mediators, 42–43, 205

O

Open minds as emotional aids, 96–98

P

Parents: reference books for, 187–90;
See also Child custody; Child sup-
port; Children; Primary caregivers
Paying bills as alimony, 182–183
Pension plans, 158
Pets as assets, 161–162
Placating as an emotional problem,
105–107
Power: appropriate use of, 93–94;
children as parental vehicles for,
119; emotional problems related
to, 103–105
Primary caregivers: in determining
child custody, 128–130; fathers as,
188–9; women as, 20–22; *See also*
Child custody; Child support; Children; Parents
Privacy in mediation, 61, 206
Property division, 165–174; after
analyzing future economic needs,
171–174; and debt assumption,
173; deciding how much each gets
in, 165–167; deciding who gets
what in, 167–170; importance of
financial analysis in, 170; liquidity
and, 173; of military benefits, 173;
overview of, 165; providing debt
security in, 173–174; of retirement
benefits, 170–171, 173; of Social
Security benefits, 173; tax conse-